An Introduction to Bibliographical and Textual Studies

By
William Proctor Williams
and
Craig S. Abbott

The Modern Language Association of America
New York   1985

Copyright ©1985 by The Modern Language Association of America

Library of Congress Cataloging in Publication Data

Williams, William Proctor, 1939-
    An introduction to bibliographical and textual studies.

    Bibliography: p.
    1. Bibliography—Methodology.   2. Criticism, Textual.   3. Transmission
of texts.   I. Abbott, Craig S., 1941–   . II. Title.
Z1001.W58   1985   010′.42   84-18975
ISBN 0-87352-133-1
ISBN 0-87352-134-X (pbk.)

Published by The Modern Language Association of America
New York, New York

Acknowledgments

After conceiving of this book and planning its coverage, Joseph McElrath of Florida State University was unable, because of other commitments, to join us in writing it. We hope that the final product comes close to matching the excellence of his initial conception.

There are also many others who can take much credit and no blame for what we offer here. For their comments and suggestions on one or more drafts, we especially thank James M. Mellard and Philip Rider, Northern Illinois University; John B. Gabel, Ohio State University, Columbus; Joel Myerson, University of South Carolina, Columbia; and the several anonymous readers for the Modern Language Association. For his suggestions as well as for his shepherding the manuscript through evaluation and revision, we thank Walter S. Achtert, Director of Book Publications and Research Programs, MLA.

Finally, for permission to reprint pages from their works, we thank several authors and publishers. Figure 4 is reprinted from *Principles of Bibliographical Description* by Fredson Bowers © 1949 by Princeton University Press. Figure 6 is reprinted from *A Bibliography of the English Printed Drama to the Restoration,* Volume II, by W. W. Greg © 1951 by Oxford University Press. Figure 7 is reprinted from *Ring W. Lardner: A Descriptive Bibliography* by Matthew J. Bruccoli and Richard Layman © 1976 by University of Pittsburgh Press. Figures 14a–14e are reprinted from *The Dramatic Works of Thomas Dekker,* Volume III, edited by Fredson Bowers © 1958 by Cambridge University Press. Figures 15a–15d are reprinted from *The Plays and Poems of Philip Massinger,* Volumes I and IV, edited by Philip Edwards and Colin Gibson © 1976 by Oxford University Press. Figures 16a–16g are reprinted from *Mardi and a Voyage Thither,* edited by Harrison Hayford, Hershel Parker, and G. Thomas Tanselle, Volume III of *The Writings of Herman Melville* © 1970 by Northwestern University Press.

William Proctor Williams
Craig S. Abbott

iii

Contents

1.

Introduction

This work provides a brief introduction to textual and bibliographical studies for both the beginning student and the more advanced scholar who has missed or avoided the subject. It is not primarily a how-to book, not a manual, but rather a guide to how this sort of scholarship has recently been and is now conducted and how its products can be applied to other branches of scholarship. We assume that most readers of this book do not intend to become bibliographers or textual critics but that they are among the principal beneficiaries of bibliography and textual criticism. Further, this is not a history of the book trade or of book production; for those subjects the reader should consult Gaskell's *A New Introduction to Bibliography* (Oxford: Oxford Univ. Press, 1972) or other specialized works listed in our reference bibliography.

We do not take a particular methodological or theoretical stance; rather, we try to describe the ways bibliographical and textual scholarship has been practiced and applied during the twentieth century. For example, we present rather full discussions of the traditional approach to the question of authorial final intention because it has been basic to critical editing since the early years of this century. But, on this question and on similar issues, we have also tried to indicate current trends, and we have provided in the notes and reference bibliography citations to major documents in the scholarly debate. Similarly, the examples that conclude the sections on descriptive bibliography and textual criticism illustrate various methods of presenting these two subjects. Although absolute neutrality is probably impossible for anyone, we have attempted to provide a road map rather than a specifically plotted route so that those who use this book may recognize areas of agreement and disagreement.

The twentieth century has seen the greatest advances in bibliographical and textual scholarship, but the subject dates back to the great library at Alexandria (founded c. 323 B.C.), which was formed primarily so that scholars might engage in textual criticism. Although the texts changed as time passed—first the Greek classics, then the Bible during the Middle Ages, and finally the Bible and the Greek and Latin classics from the Renaissance on—the methods

1

employed were solely concerned with a manuscript textual tradition for which a long history existed. In the nineteenth century, when English literature began to be established as an academic discipline, it was only natural that those scholars who took up English studies should apply the methods of classical textual criticism to English texts, for they had all been educated in a traditional classical school system. But a few nineteenth-century editors of the English classics practiced a seemingly whimsical eclecticism, and their method sometimes resembled Lancelot Andrewes' preaching as described in John Aubrey's *Brief Lives*: "he did play with his text, as a Jack-an-apes does, who takes up a thing and tosses and plays with it, and then takes up another, and plays a little with it. Here's a pretty thing and there's a pretty thing!" At times their editorial work consisted of picking a convenient previous printing and then adding their commentary notes. The nineteenth century did witness some notable attempts, such as the Variorum Shakespeare, to prepare sound editions based on the best methods of the times. Although most nineteenth-century editors were sincere and diligent, Stanley Wells's assessment of eighteenth- and nineteenth-century work on Shakespeare is not unjust:

> The work of these early editors was carried out in relative ignorance of the theatrical and printing conditions that prevailed in Shakespeare's day; ... the emendations they made were governed by literary, grammatical and linguistic standards of their time and by the stylistic and theatrical tastes of individual editors [and] ... while the 'good' and 'bad' quartos received a great deal of attention and use, scholarly opinion had not really crystallized into any settled view of their varying claims to authority.[1]

On the less austere side of things were editors like Henry Morley, who claimed he had edited the many hundreds of works reprinted in the 209 volumes of *Cassell's National Library* (1888–89).

At the beginning of the twentieth century a group of scholars—W. W. Greg, R. B. McKerrow, F. P. Wilson, A. W. Pollard, and others—began to study the texts of Shakespeare and his contemporary dramatists in a way that came to be known as the New Bibliography. This new methodology was grounded on a firm and ever more thorough understanding of the book as a physical object and involved studying the operation of the book trade, the technical procedures of setting, printing, proofing, binding, and selling books. The New Bibliographers rediscovered what the classical and biblical textual critic had always known: in the real-time history of a text, the only moment that reveals any information about the correct form of the text is that moment when it moves from one form to another and from which the later form survives. This is the case whether the transmission involves a scribe listening to the dictation of a text by a fellow worker and moving an inked pen across sheets of parchment or a compositor looking at an author's manuscript and placing individual pieces of type into a composing stick from which they are transferred to a chase and then to the press for printing. Where some earlier English editors had gone wrong was in neglecting the ways texts have been transmitted and in viewing the text as an abstraction with a life of its own outside of real time and space.

With the rapid growth in the study of English and American literature in the years following World War I, this physical examination of the text, the documents that contained it, and its genetics gradually spread beyond the confines of English Renaissance drama into almost all literature in English and, to a lesser extent, literature in the other modern European languages. This expansion in bibliographical studies and their application to textual criticism were certainly spurred by the discovery that many major works suffered from textual corruption. Increasingly, scholars desired to read literature in the words the authors wrote, purged of the corruptions inherent in hand copying or typesetting and those willfully introduced by families, friends, and well-intentioned publishers' editors. The value and methods of bibliographical and textual studies have not gone unquestioned, however. Even so sophisticated a critic as Edmund Wilson attacked the way textual criticism was applied to the works of American authors in the Center for Editions of American Authors project, and similar, though sometimes more cogent, questions have come from the ranks of editors themselves.[2] This debate, if it has generated some confusion, has also had the beneficial effect of forcing editors to examine their assumptions, aims, and methods. Moreover, even those who have questioned particular editorial methods have benefited from the wealth of information discovered during the editorial process—information bearing on authors' styles and methods of composition; on the evolution of particular texts; on the profession of authorship in various periods; on economic, political, and technological influences on texts; and on literary history generally.

We hope that this book, by describing the aims and methods of bibliographical and textual scholars, will make more accessible the fruits of their endeavors. Readers should understand that ours is primarily a rhetoric of description and summary, not of personal discovery. Throughout, we rely on the work of many scholars. Although we provide citations for some references within our text, we cannot possibly cite every important piece of scholarship bearing on what we present. While our notes can acknowledge specific debts, they cannot acknowledge many greater and more pervasive ones. For these works and for essential further sources of information, readers should consult our reference bibliography.

TEXTS

The basic commodity for a literary scholar is the text, which is physically embodied in letters written, impressed, or transferred onto a surface. It is not possible to speak of light and dark imagery in *Richard III*, "Necessity and the Role of the Hero in Shelley's *Prometheus Unbound*," or the literary criticism of Edmund Wilson unless one starts with the marks on the paper that present the text. No matter what else we may know about authors, we must always refer our views back to the texts they have left us. Hence, although bibliographical studies are popularly thought to be distinct from critical studies, the two are in truth sides of the same coin. One does not normally perform extensive bibliographical work on the *Guiness Book of World Records* or the New York City telephone directory, because these are not literary texts. Indeed, until recently one did not perform extensive bibliographic studies on historical or philosophical texts, though it would appear that this neglect is being remedied.

Texts have lives. They are the products of people's minds and hands and are thus in a real sense historical, whether we are dealing with the life of Shakespeare's *Othello* (from the First Quarto of 1622 to the most recent paperback published for classroom use, over none of which the author exercised any direct control) or with that of Marianne Moore's "Poetry" (which began its public life in 1919 as thirty lines, went through stages of thirteen, fifteen, and twenty-nine lines, and ended its life in 1967 as three lines, Moore herself evidently being responsible for all these alterations). Certainly the student of Shakespeare or Moore cannot use any text that comes to hand, cannot merely browse through the library or bookstore stacks and take the copy that hasn't been checked out or sold, nor can the teacher select just any textbook for use in class. *The Norton Anthology of Poetry* (rev. ed.; New York: Norton, 1975) prints the version of "Poetry" that is twenty-nine lines long, with no indication that there are other versions of other lengths. Similarly, in Auden's later editions of his "complete" poems, one will not find his "September First 1939." And then there are the almost supernatural vicissitudes of Chapters 28 and 29 of James's *The Ambassadors*, which were reversed in the first American edition in 1903 and in all subsequent American editions until 1955. At this point the publishers, Harper and Brothers, announced that theirs would be the first American edition with the chapters in the correct order, but they were not. In 1957 Harper finally published an edition with Chapter 28 coming before Chapter 29, but in 1958, after Harper leased the rights to Doubleday, the Doubleday Anchor paperback came out with Chapter 29 again ahead of Chapter 28! It probably also makes a difference whether Linco in Richard Fanshawe's translation of *Il Pastor Fido* says "Leave, leave the woods, leave following beasts, fond boy, / And follow Love" (as he does, correctly, in the 1647 and 1648 editions) or "Love, leave the woods, leave following beasts, fond boy, / and follow Love" (as he does, incorrectly, in the 1664, 1676, 1692, and 1736 editions).[3]

Texts, as we have said, have physical embodiments. Certainly the literary work begins in the mind of the author, but since that form is inaccessible, the author must set pen to paper or fingers to typewriter or must dictate for a typist. Errors will result from the making of this first physical embodiment of the text (the manuscript or typescript). Almost all authors will then produce revised manuscripts, drafts, recastings, foul papers, fair copies, and the like. Eventually, if a work makes its way to the printer and publisher, further textual alteration will occur. Before English spelling became regularized (roughly, with Johnson's *Dictionary* in 1755), compositors spelled many words according to their personal tastes, and they could also make spelling alterations to justify full lines of verse or prose. Thus, compositors might set *do* or *doe, go* or *goe, catholic* or *catholick* or *catholique.* They might also differ in how they spaced around punctuation, displayed headings, and dealt with lines of verse too long for their composing sticks. In all these permitted and seemingly inconsequential ways compositors could produce yet one more version of the author's text. Compositors were also known to generate more striking alterations either because they thought their setting copy was wrong or because they could not make it out and were forced to guess. A probable instance is the famous textual crux in the First Folio (1623) edition of Shakespeare's *Henry V* where the Hostesse, describing Falstaff's death, says, "for his Nose was as sharpe as a Pen, and a Table of greene fields" (ll. 838–39). It is commonly thought today that the compositor at this point could not read the manuscript, which probably read "a babld [babbled] of greene fields," and produced a version of the text that is not what Shakespeare wrote and that makes little or no sense.

Since the standardization of spelling, compositors have not been allowed the luxury of varying the author's spelling of common words (unless the author spells unconventionally) but have managed to perpetrate various sins of omission and commission on the texts they have set in type. Anyone who has ever spent time reading proofs will have countless examples of the transpositions, omissions, repetitions, and the like produced by compositors. The sorts of errors may change as technology changes. Hand setting in the nineteenth century produced different missettings than does computer composing in the late twentieth. But the dicta of W. W. Greg in *The Calculus of Variants* (Oxford: Clarendon, 1927) that "the process of transcription is characterized by variation" and that "such variation may be assumed to be universal, every transcription introducing some variants . . . in all but the shortest texts" (p. 8) hold true no matter by what means a text passes from one form to another.

Authors—and authors' agents (copy editors, correctors for the press who check or are supposed to check proofs against copy, secretaries, spouses, friends, and literary executors)—have regularly been given the opportunity to correct texts in proof or in subsequent editions. Charlton Hinman has demonstrated that as early as 1623, Shakespeare's works in the First Folio were rather carelessly proofed in places, probably by Jaggard, the printer. And since the late eighteenth century it has been a regular part of the publication process to supply the author with proofs. However, not only has bibliographical study shown that reading proofs does not remove all the variants introduced by the printing process, but it has also demonstrated that the very process of proofreading, revising by the author during proofreading, and making the proof corrections in the type or plates introduces further errors and thus creates other forms of the text.

Clearly, a doctrine of textual original sin should be one of the creedal statements of literary scholars. Not only do all texts have lives, but these lives tend to go from bad to worse, and like any prudent single person, the literary critic will be well advised to inquire into the past life of a text before wedding it!

From what we have just said it should be evident that bibliography and textual criticism are anterior to literary criticism and that the scholar's first job is to study the text's physical embodiments and mode of transmission or, if that job has already been done by other scholars, to scrutinize facts and opinions already demonstrated. Thus even those who do not engage in bibliographical and textual scholarship themselves must know how to use its products: bibliographies, histories of printing and publishing, critical editions, and so forth. Within this scholarship there are a number of subdivisions, each offering material valuable to all literary students.

ANALYTICAL BIBLIOGRAPHY

This branch of bibliographical investigation, often used as an umbrella term to cover all forms of physical bibliography, concerns the physical embodiments of texts as evidence of the process that produced these embodiments and of the relations between them. For analytical bibliographers the book is a physical object, and it is examined in ways similar to those employed in any other examination of a physical object, by, say, a geologist, botanist, or criminal investigator. Analytical bibliographers try to determine the date and method of composition, the source and nature of the compositors' copy, the identity and proclivities of the compositors, and the kind and quantity of type or the kind of machine used in composition. In the period of hand printing (approximately before 1800) they will want to know when and in what order the pages of type were imposed, sent to the press, and then washed, rinsed, and distributed back into the type cases. In the period after 1800 they will want to know whether stereotype or other kinds of plates were made and how these plates were subsequently corrected and used. They will want to know how the book was exposed to the public (whether it was sold or given away, how many copies from what sources were issued at a specific time). In the modern era they will study the book's binding and dust jacket as well as the book itself. Finally, they will usually want to ask these questions about all books by a particular author, about all books with a particular title, or about a particular kind of book. Thus they will examine all copies of books by Fielding, all copies of *Tom Jones*, or all eighteenth-century English novels. They will have no direct concern, while practicing analytical bibliography, with what any of the books say but will be totally concerned with how they came to be—the embodiments should *be*, not mean!

It is this branch of bibliography that has taken most of the abuse from the tongues and pens of fellow scholars and critics. This opposition reflects the attackers' failure to see—and the bibliographers' failure to demonstrate—the necessity of such investigation. The objective and disinterested examination of books as physical objects feeds the other branches of bibliography and, in turn, helps produce the raw material for the study of literature. The analytical studies of just one book, the First Folio of Shakespeare's works, by Charlton Hinman, Trevor Howard-Hill, Andrew Cairncross, W. W. Greg, and many others have produced often startling results, the implications of which extend not only to the text of Shakespeare's works but to any work printed during the same era. All this information, with obvious applications to other sorts of bibliography and also to literary studies generally, was uncovered by analytical bibliographers, who came on it by considering books only as physical objects. It is unlikely that investigators who treated the First Folio in any other way would have found it, as they would not have been looking for physical evidence. The First Folio regarded as a literary treasure of the English language, which it certainly is, will not yield the same evidence as does the First Folio studied as a book produced according to certain physical processes, just like those used to produce an almanac for 1623 or an herbal, that can be analyzed by anyone with a clear understanding of how type gets impressed into paper.

HISTORICAL BIBLIOGRAPHY

As its name implies, this branch of bibliography concerns itself with the history of the book. Usually it treats either printing history (the study of the methods of setting and printing employed in the past) or book-trade history (the methods of sale and distribution and the organization of the book trade employed in the past). Historical bibliographers may concentrate their efforts on a particular publisher, printer, bookseller, binder, or typefounder, or they may devote themselves to the study of paper, type, presses of a particular make or style, bindings, and similar matters. Some work in this field, however, takes larger concerns for its subject and may discuss such matters as the impact of printing on Western culture, the cultural impact of the transition from manuscript to print, the effect of a mass literary market on literary standards, or, more recently, the effect of electronic data processing on language and literature. This broader view of historical bibliography, often termed *l'histoire du livre,* may be seen, for example, in Lucien Febvre and Henri-Jean Martin's influential *L'Apparition du Livre* (1958), a study not merely of printing history but primarily of the impact of the book on civilization through the end of the eighteenth century.[4]

Obviously, much of the information provided by historical bibliography is used by analytical bibliography and thence by other branches of the subject. Also, it is as much a subdivision of history as it is of bibliography.

REFERENCE BIBLIOGRAPHY

To the general public, the most familiar kind of bibliography is a list of works compiled according to some style sheet such as the *MLA Handbook* or *The*

Chicago Manual of Style. The art of compiling such lists (as well as the lists themselves) is called reference bibliography or systematic bibliography. It focuses less on books (or periodicals or whatever) as physical objects than on the works contained in them. A reference bibliography that is merely a list is an enumerative bibliography; one that includes abstracts, summaries, or descriptions of the works is an annotated bibliography. Annotated or enumerative, such a bibliography is the product of a principle of selection, method of citation, and system of organization that require careful thought and difficult decisions. Many reference bibliographies are among the standard tools of scholarship—for example, the *Cumulative Book Index*, *New Cambridge Bibliography of English Literature*, *MLA International Bibliography*, MHRA *Annual Bibliography of English Language and Literature*, and *Abstracts of English Studies*. The subject of reference bibliography is beyond the scope of this work and will not be discussed further.

DESCRIPTIVE BIBLIOGRAPHY

Most other branches of bibliography make considerable use of the results of analytical bibliography. Descriptive bibliography does so because it presents an orderly, usually chronological description of the physical embodiments of texts. Normally its subject is a physical description of all the books containing works by a single author, perhaps within a given time span, or all the books of a particular type. From an examination of particular copies, it produces an ideal description of a book—a historical reconstruction of the book as the publisher exposed it to the public—and it records all the variants from this ideal form.

The purpose of descriptive bibliography is twofold. First, it tries to record all the forms in which a particular book may be found so that a subsequent scholar or critic will know what is wrong or right about the copy at hand. In other words, it serves as a means of identification. Second, it provides a norm against which other copies, unknown or unexamined at the time the bibliography was prepared, may be checked. The surviving copies of a novel published in 1936 are so numerous that the examination of all copies is not usually possible, and one copy in a library in a remote corner of Wyoming or New York City may contain a significant variant in physical form. For the books of earlier periods, unrecorded copies are constantly being unearthed, and they too may contain variants.

Descriptive bibliography differs from analytical bibliography only because its aim is different. Though both are concerned with the book as physical object, analytical bibliography attempts to anatomize the process that brought the book into being, while descriptive bibliography seeks to describe accurately the object produced by the process and all the variations caused by alterations in the process. In methodology and terminology the two fields are nearly identical.

TEXTUAL CRITICISM

Textual criticism, the oldest branch of bibliographical scholarship, is the study of the transmission of texts. Its aim is to trace the history of texts and to establish sound texts according to certain principles and using certain methods, which vary from period to period of history. The focus here is the text itself rather than its physical embodiments, but obviously no text exists apart from a physical embodiment. Hence, textual criticism uses many of the findings of analytical and descriptive bibliography. For example, if analytical and descriptive bibliography discover that the gatherings of a Jacobean play quarto were set in series ("seriatim"), this information indicates to the textual critic a range of possible explanations for textual variations that occur early or late in a particular gathering. More obviously, the evidence of analytical and descriptive bibliography assists the textual critic in determining the correctness of textual alterations made during the printing of a book.

Such direct application of analytical bibliography to textual questions is usually called textual bibliography. Textual criticism must also deal with the relations between different versions of a text produced over a period of time—normally, successive editions in the period of printing. Analytical or descriptive bibliography can help here as well. For example, these two fields have solved the question of the supposed first edition of Sir John Davies' *Nosce Teipsum* (1599) by demonstrating from physical evidence that before the first quarto had been completed and sold, a line-for-line resetting of the work had begun and that early on copies appeared containing mixed sheets from these two settings.[5] Textual critics, without the aid of analytical and descriptive bibliography, might eventually have guessed at the answer, but it is far more likely that they would never have produced a sound text. However, often these other processes cannot aid textual criticism in its final decisions, and it is here especially that the critical scholarly mind must be brought to bear on textual variants. Many different systems for dealing with such questions have been devised, and several will be discussed in later sections of this book. Textual critics have relied on lexical rules (authors cannot use a word that did not exist at the time they were writing), metrical rules (in works with regular metrical patterns, nonmetrical readings are judged inferior), genetic relationships of texts (the diagramming of a group of texts in patterns resembling family trees), and quasi-mathematical ordering of texts (a calculuslike arrangement of variant patterns in texts such as the systems devised by Greg and Dearing; see the reference bibliography).

But modern textual criticism is still most notable for its reliance, whenever possible, on physical evidence. It may often be convenient for the literary critic in all of us to wish that our text read a particular way, but the textual critic must render the text the way the author wrote it. For example, a reviewer of Roger Sale's *Modern Heroism* in the *Times Literary Supplement* (27 July

1973, p. 848) pointed out that William Empson had "mutilated" a passage from Pope's *Moral Epistle IV* when he quoted it in *Seven Types of Ambiguity* thus:

> Another age shall see the golden ear
> Embrown the slope, and nod on the parterre,
> Deep harvest [sic] bury all his pride has planned,
> And laughing Ceres reassume the land.

We all fail to copy accurately from time to time (see Greg's principle of universal variation, p. 5), but William Empson responded by indulging in the sort of textual criticism that the twentieth century has ceased to value. He said, in a subsequent issue of the *TLS*, that the *s* had been dropped from "harvests" in the Courthope and Everyman editions (1881 and 1924 respectively) and so

> in this case it was the sensitive Victorians, and not I, who had divined the true text. There can be little doubt that Pope first wrote our version and only printed the prosy one out of timidity.... I think that a later Complete Edition would be justified in putting 'Courthope, *harvest*' into its Apparatus.

The reviewer's response is a fine statement, where Empson's is not, of what modern textual criticism is about.

> I am sorry that Professor Empson has been misled by inferior texts. F. W. Bateson's Twickenham Edition (which is based on the 1744 "death-bed" edition and takes into account the nine previous editions or reprints) gives "harvests" in the plural and lists no singular variant in its *apparatus criticus*. I cannot see any reason to add a "sensitive" emendation which depends on the doubtful editorial procedure of divination. I have no such way of being certain about ... the working of his [Pope's] mind. Neither has Professor Empson—but what Pope actually wrote seems the safest indication. (*TLS*, 24 August 1973, p. 978)

This is precisely the point of textual criticism: to present an authoritative text based on a full study of the text's transmission through manuscript and print. Though textual critics may propose emendations, these must also be based on that study and not on a mere feeling that a particular reading is better and therefore is the author's.

Scholarly editing may take a number of forms, ranging from the faithful transcription of a particular state of a text (that found in a particular document) to a historical reconstruction of a text as its author intended it. This latter form, critical editing, has dominated contemporary textual criticism. It involves the textual critic in several matters, some bibliographical and some critical. Thus textual critics must be textually acute, possessing a full knowledge of analytical, descriptive, historical, and textual bibliography and their applications; but they must also be critically acute, with a full knowledge of literary history, philology, poetic or prosaic stylistics, the structure of given works in a given period, and the characteristics of the author in question.

2.

Analytical Bibliography

Analytical bibliography attempts to determine the printing history of books by examining them physically. Like detective work (indeed, it has forensic applications), it combines drudgery with excitement and can turn up bits of information that, though seemingly minor, may have considerable significance. As a discipline, analytical bibliography developed largely through the study of textual problems in English Renaissance drama. By 1958, although the field was still young (having flowered only in the twentieth century in work by such scholars as W. W. Greg, R. B. McKerrow, Alice Walker, Charlton Hinman, and Fredson Bowers), Bowers could justly warn "that when the evidence of analytical bibliography is available, critical judgment must be limited by bibliographical probabilities and must never run contrary to bibliographical findings."[6] If Bowers' warning indicates the importance of analytical bibliography, it also recognizes the limits. Bibliography may provide evidence and findings that the critic, textual or otherwise, cannot ignore, but it does not replace critical judgment. Using watermarks, type batter, press variants, spelling habits, running titles, and the like, the bibliographer may establish the date of a book, identify the compositors who set its pages, and determine the sequence of variant states of the parts. The textual critic must take these findings into account, but they do not themselves perform the editorial function.

The focus on textual problems has both helped and hindered analytical bibliography. It has provided justification for what some might otherwise label as mere pedantry and has forced bibliographers to see their endeavors in relation to other areas, literary and historical. Yet the focus also has tended to obscure the independence of bibliography as a discipline that can illuminate not only the printing of a particular literary work but also the whole history of printing and the history of the book as an instrument and product of human culture.

The primary evidence in analytical bibliography is that of the books themselves. While this evidence may be certain, the conclusions based on it—or hypotheses constructed to explain it—are often uncertain. As Bowers has

11

pointed out, they range from the demonstrable to the probable to the merely possible. Insufficient evidence and ignorance of conflicting evidence plague bibliography just as they do any field. And as D. F. McKenzie has demonstrated, bibliographers at times have based conclusions on questionable assumptions about the normality and regularity of printing-house practices.[7]

Not all evidence found in books is primary, for books often make statements about themselves. Title pages, for example, often list dates, printers, publishers, and the like, but this secondary evidence is not always reliable. Misinformation may appear by accident: the earliest date in an English printed book, M. CCCC. LXVIII (1468), is now recognized as a misprint for M. CCCC. LXXVIII (1478). Or it may appear through subterfuge: E. B. Browning's *The Runaway Slave at Pilgrim's Point*, despite its title page, was not published by Chapman and Hall in 1849; the book is a forgery by T. J. Wise and was probably printed in 1888. Or it may appear for as yet undetermined reasons: the Warner paperpack of Carl Bernstein and Bob Woodward's *All the President's Men* claiming to be the "First Printing: February, 1975" was available from retail bookstores at least as early as 17 December 1974.

Other secondary evidence derives from a wide variety of sources. The records and archives of printers and publishers, for example, are invaluable, and some have been deposited in research libraries. Records of copyright often contain information on the date, authorship, and manufacture of books. Many of these are available in print: *A Transcript of the Registers of the Company of Stationers* (i.e., of the guild that controlled the English book trade) has been edited for the years 1554–1640 by Edward Arber (1875–94; rpt. Gloucester, Mass.: Peter Smith, 1967) and for 1640–1708 by George E. B. Eyre (1913–14; rpt. Gloucester, Mass.: Peter Smith, 1950), and a record of American copyrights since 1891 appears in the *Catalog of Copyright Entries*. Similarly useful are the publishing industry's trade lists, such as the *Term Catalogues, 1668–1709*, edited by Edward Arber, and the well-known *Publishers' Trade List Annual* (1874–) and *Books in Print* (1948–). For an understanding of printing methods used during various periods, analytical bibliographers consult contemporary printers' manuals, such as Joseph Moxon's *Mechanick Exercises on the Whole Art of Printing* (London, 1683–84) and W. Savage's *A Dictionary of the Art of Printing* (London, 1841). And they consult retrospective studies of book production and trade, such as R. B. McKerrow's *A Dictionary of Printers and Booksellers in England, Scotland, and Ireland, and of Foreign Printers of English Books, 1557–1640* (London: Bibliographical Soc., 1910), Daniel B. Updike's *Printing Types: Their History, Forms, and Use*, 3rd ed. (Cambridge: Belknap–Harvard Univ. Press, 1962), James Moran's *Printing Presses: History and Development from the Fifteenth Century to Modern Times* (Berkeley: Univ. of California Press, 1973), Rollo Silver's *The American Printer, 1787–1825* (Charlottesville: Univ. Press of Virginia, 1967), and Marjorie Plant's *The English Book Trade: An Economic History of the Making and Sale of Books*,

2nd ed. (London: Allen & Unwin, 1965). In other words, the vast body of material for the study of the history of books—their materials, manufacture, and sale—has obvious relevance for analytical bibliography.

Among the sources of physical evidence are the ingredients and form of paper. The manufacture of book paper requires some type of fibers and a sizing to hold the fibers and prevent the feathering of wet ink. Coatings, pigments, and fillers of various types may also be added. Microscopy can sometimes identify the kind of fibers or fillers used in a particular sample of paper, and relatively simple chemical tests can reveal these and other constituents as well. For example, a solution of phloroglucinol dropped on a piece of paper reveals the presence of mechanically pulped wood fibers by reacting with their lignin and turning red or magenta, the deepness of the color serving as a rough indication of the amount present. Similar tests can detect alum, rosin, starch, animal glue, and casein. In addition to differentiating between two stocks of paper, these tests may establish the earliest date a paper, and thus a book, could have been manufactured, because it is known when certain ingredients were introduced in papermaking: for instance, soda wood pulp in 1845, mechanical wood pulp in 1869, esparto grass in 1861, chemically pulped wood in 1874, rosin in 1835, clay filler in 1870.[8]

Such qualitative analysis of paper served John Carter and Graham Pollard in their well-known exposure of the forgeries of T. J. Wise.[9] Among the activities, respectable and not, to which Wise devoted his skill was the forgery of more than fifty pamphlets containing works by Ruskin, Swinburne, Tennyson, Kipling, the Brownings, and others. Dated earlier than previous publications of the works and appearing in limited editions, these pamphlets fetched handsome prices in the rare-book trade and made their way into standard bibliographies of these authors' works, some of the bibliographies being compiled by Wise himself. Carter and Pollard discovered that though esparto grass was not used in book papers before 1861 and chemical wood pulp not before 1874, some of the pamphlets bearing earlier dates had been printed on paper containing these ingredients. E. B. Browning's *Runaway Slave*, for example, could not have been printed in 1849, as its title page claimed, for its paper could not have been manufactured until some time after 1874.

Papermaking processes also leave their traces. Until the early nineteenth century, book paper was handmade, produced with sievelike molds dipped into vats of pulped rags. The molds were rectangular frames with closely spaced wires running lengthwise and larger wires ("chains") running across at intervals of about twenty-five millimeters. One can see this pattern of wires if one holds such paper (called "laid" paper) up to the light. Usually also visible are watermarks, which were created when designs were fixed with wire into the center of one half of the mold. (Beginning in the sixteenth century, extra marks, called "countermarks," were sometimes placed in the other half of the mold.) In the early nineteenth century, "wove" paper became common. It was first made by hand, with molds that used a woven wire mesh. Shortly thereafter, wove paper was made by machine, to which was sometimes attached a dandy roll that imposed watermarks and even what look like wire and chain lines.

Because watermarks and countermarks were used variously (at various times) to indicate the papermill, size of sheet, quality of paper, and date of manufacture, they are obvious bits of bibliographical evidence and are recoverable even from heavily printed sheets by a beta-radiographic process.[10] In the early years of the New Bibliography, for example, investigations by Pollard, Greg, and William Neidig proved that a number of Shakespeare's quartos bore false dates. The presence of identical watermarks in quartos dated 1600, 1608, and 1619, when combined with other physical evidence, indicated that the suspect quartos had all been printed in 1619 by Pavier.[11] Until the revelation, some of the misdated quartos had been regarded as first editions or as editions derived from rival manuscripts.

A more complex use of watermark evidence is found in A. H. Stevenson's *The Problem of the Missale Speciale* (London: Bibliographical Soc., 1967). A missal, often called the Constance Missal, had been the subject of great controversy since the first description of a copy in 1898. Many scholars thought it to predate the Psalter of 1457 and even the Gutenberg Bible of 1455, making it possibly the earliest extant book printed from movable type. Others, using typographical or liturgical evidence, offered dates ranging up to the 1480s. Although there had been some mention of paper evidence, it was not used with thoroughness and understanding until Stevenson's investigation. Examining the four extant copies of the missal, Stevenson identified its paper molds through the watermarks and the sewing dots that showed where the watermarks had been attached to the wires and chains of the molds. Finding paper from the same molds in eleven other books, all from the 1470s, Stevenson narrowed the possible range of dates. Then, tracing the variant states of the watermarks in the missal and other books—states resulting from deterioration of the marks— and joining this evidence with that of colophons, rubrication dates, type styles, bindings, and liturgical history, he arrived at the date of 1473.

The other principal kind of physical evidence is that of type—or, more accurately, the inked impressions made by type or plates. Ink itself has been little used in analytical bibliography. Its potential, though, can be seen in the example of the so-called Vinland map of 1400, which was for some time thought to prove that Norsemen had discovered North America before Columbus did. Microanalysis of its ink demonstrated that the map was a fake, since it contained an ingredient first used in ink in the 1920s. More recently, cyclotron analysis has been employed to determine the chemical "fingerprints" of ink in early books. But the image, not the ink, has chiefly concerned bibliographers. It is, for example, a clue to the printing process used in a book. Under a hand lens, an image printed by type or relief plates has edges containing a ring of ink; by gravure, edges that are serrated; and by offset, edges that are smooth and evenly inked. The image is also, so to speak, the fingerprint of the type used to create it: it identifies the type and ornaments. Records of various fonts and styles of type used in particular times and places sometimes appear in type-specimen books, in studies of type and typefounders, and indirectly, of course, in other books using the same kind of type. Moreover, especially in the early handpress period, printers' woodcut ornaments and to some extent even their stocks of type tended to be unique, thus serving to identify their work. Identification of both a type font and a printer's unique stock assisted Carter and Pollard in exposing the Wise forgeries. Some sixteen suspect pamphlets employed a kernless type—that is, a type in which the ascending or descending portions of letters like *f* and *j* do not extend beyond the body of the type. Though bearing dates of 1842 through 1873, the pamphlets must have been printed after 1883, when such kernless type came into use. Carter and Pollard also noticed that the type used in some pamphlets, such as E. B. Browning's *Sonnets* ("1847"), came from a mixed font: to the kernless type had been added a peculiar question mark from another font. This mixed font probably belonged only to one printer. Finding it also present in a reprint of Matthew Arnold's *Alaric at Rome* (1893), Carter and Pollard concluded that its printer, Richard Clay and Sons Ltd., had also printed the spurious pamphlets.

The other major source of primary evidence, in addition to the materials of the book, is that left by the processes of composition (setting the type), imposition (arranging the pages of type for the printing of sheets), proofing (finding and correcting errors of composition), and presswork (printing of the sheets). Some of the traces left by these processes may be inadvertent, but they are nonetheless useful. A "new edition" of Byron's *Don Juan*, Cantos 1 and 2, bears the date 1822 and the imprint of John Murray. But on the verso of the title page in at least one copy, there is faintly printed another title page— one from an 1824 edition of Cantos 15 and 16 and with the imprint of John Hunt. How did this happen? We know that after printing one side of a sheet (or stack of sheets) and before printing the other side, a printer would have to let the ink set or use additional sheets to protect the press; otherwise, the printed image would be transferred to the tympan (a parchment-backed frame used to hold the sheet when printing) and then be set off onto the next sheet printed. Setoff might also result from contact of two sheets. Such setoff evidently occurred when the supposed 1822 edition and the 1824 edition were being printed concurrently. Unable to publish legally the first five cantos because Murray held the copyright, Hunt resorted to piracy. The 1822 edition is actually an 1824 edition, and it is Hunt's, not Murray's.[12]

Using the evidence left by the processes of production requires a knowledge of when, where, and how the processes were employed and of the possible significance of deviations from "normal" practice. Certain habits or practices of composition, for example, are peculiar to particular times and places. Even the bibliographically uninitiated recognize the long *s* (*ʃ*) as uncharacteristic of modern printing, since it died out in the late eighteenth and early nineteenth centuries. It is used occasionally nowadays, to provide a cultivated quaintness, but it is likely to reveal itself as modern. A few years ago, a restaurant called the Fyfe and Drum sought to enhance its Revolutionary War atmosphere by sporting long *s* in its menus. The prices alone served to date the menu, of course, but the long *s* was fishy too. The modern compositor had used it throughout, unaware that earlier printers used short *s* at the ends of words and generally before the letters *b, k,* and *f.* Another obvious example of differences in compositorial (or editorial) practice is that between British and American style. A recent book with the spellings *honour, arse,* and *connexion,* with single quotation marks enclosing simple quotations, and with periods and commas occurring outside the closing quotation mark (at least when not part of the quotation) was probably set into type in England rather than in the United States. Similarly but somewhat less obviously, as R. A. Sayce has shown, compositors' practices in setting catchwords, signatures, page numbers, and dates can identify the locality and period in which a book was printed.[13] For example, a handpress book with page numbers enclosed in square brackets is almost certainly English and probably of the eighteenth century, while one with numbers enclosed in ornaments is almost certainly German.

Another kind of compositor study seeks to identify the compositor or compositors who set the type for some book or books. Until spelling began to be standardized in the mid-eighteenth century, compositors spelled according to their tastes and felt no great need to preserve the spelling of their copy. While one compositor in a printshop might prefer such spellings as *sweete, young, traytor, mistresse,* and *suddenly,* another might prefer *sweet, yong, traitor, mistris,* and *sodainely.* Compositors' habits could also differ in the abbreviation of dramatic speech prefixes, in the punctuation of abbreviations, in the use of italic (e.g., for names in a roman text), in spacing before and after punctuation, in the lineation of verse, in capitalization, and in the placement of signatures on pages. Compositor study is greatly aided—and its textual applications become clearer—when compositors' work can be compared to the copy that they followed. Such comparison reveals the compositors' level and kind of accuracy—the extent to which they were prone to substitution, omission, transposition, and "correction." This knowledge is of obvious use to the textual critic who must decide whether and how to emend a text set by a particular compositor.

Composition cannot be isolated from imposition or for that matter from the other processes of book production. If we assume, for example, that efficient production would require a balance between composition and presswork, then the method of doing one would directly affect the other. Otherwise, the press and its operators would stand idle while the compositors worked, and vice versa. To some extent, then, imposition mediates between composition and presswork. As such it reflects backward to reveal how, by whom, and in what order the pages of type were composed, and it reflects forward to reveal the order in which the formes (or assembled type pages) were printed, the possibility of delays in printing, and the extent and method of proofing. Imposition is the arrangement of pages of set type within a rectangular frame called a chase so that a sheet printed from the arrangement could be folded to produce a gathering (or part of a gathering) with its pages in the correct order. We discuss various schemes of imposition in our section on descriptive bibliography. Here, though, we can use the example of one scheme for imposing sheets in quarto. Since a sheet of paper has two sides, our scheme requires two formes, the "outer" forme for pages 1, 4, 5, and 8 and the "inner" forme for pages 2, 3, 6, and 7:

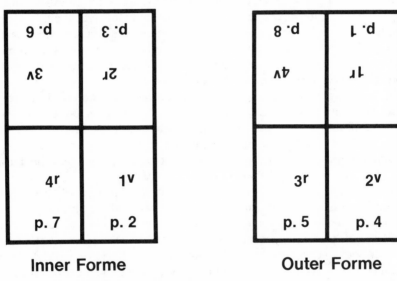

Inner Forme   **Outer Forme**

Fig. 1.   Imposition for a sheet in quarto.

Around each set of type pages would be fixed a "skeleton" forme—that is, the chase in which the type pages were locked up for printing, the wooden "furniture" used to hold the type, the wedges ("quoins") used to tighten the fit, and the typographical matter used in the headlines, including running titles and page numbers.

Although our quarto would require two formes for printing, it would not necessarily require two chases or two sets of headlines and wooden furniture— or, in the printer's jargon, two skeletons. For after printing from one forme, the printer could rinse the skeleton and then use it to enclose the other. An examination of headlines indicates that some books were printed with but one skeleton, others with two or more. The clue to the number of skeletons used in printing a book, then, is the number of sets of headlines, since a set of headlines would migrate with the skeleton as it was used in a sequence of formes. The individual headlines, at least in pre-nineteenth-century books, can often be identified—and their recurrence throughout the sheets of the book traced—by their spelling, capitalization, punctuation, spacing, type font, or broken or otherwise unique pieces of type. A headline used in page 2 of an inner forme might reappear on page 4 of the outer forme of the same sheet if the book was printed with one skeleton. Of course, using but one skeleton would cause delay. Unless some other book was being printed concurrently, the press would be idle while the skeleton was rinsed and transferred to the next forme. To avoid delay, the printer might use two skeletons (and thus two sets of headlines), one for each forme of a sheet. These two sets can also be traced through a book. The skeleton used for the inner forme might appear again on the inner forme of the next sheet, and so on. Analytical bibliography attempts to determine the pattern in which headlines occur, to detect deviations from the pattern—deviations of headline position within successive formes, of the whole set in the sequence, and within individual headlines—and to draw various conclusions from the pattern and deviations.

If, for example, the pattern of headline recurrence in a book indicates two skeletons, the bibliographer can make tentative conclusions about the proofing that the book may have undergone (and thus about the accuracy of the text and the kinds of emendations that an editor may or may not have to make). Collating multiple copies of such a book may reveal that, in every sheet, one forme (i.e., one side of the sheet) contains textual variants indicating proof correction, while the other forme is invariant. This pattern of variant and invariant formes, coinciding with the pattern of two-skeleton printing, may be quite regular, as when all inner formes bear textual variants and all outer formes lack them. This pattern might seem to suggest that, for some reason, the outer formes did not undergo proof correction. But more likely they did. In "Elizabethan Proofing," Fredson Bowers outlines the printing and proofing sequence that produced sheets made up of variant and invariant formes in two-skeleton printing.[14] After imposition, the first sheet printed from the inner forme would be used for proofing, but *printing continued until the proofing was completed.* At that time, the forme would be removed from the press and corrected. Meanwhile, the outer forme, which was being imposed while the inner forme was being printed, was placed on the press and a sheet printed for proofing. It was removed from the press for correction and replaced by the corrected inner forme for further printing. The outer forme was corrected and returned to the press after the printing of the inner forme. Thus the presence of invariant formes does not rule out proofing. In our example, both formes were proofed, but only one (the inner) would show proof correction because only it was at one stage printed in an uncorrected state.

The analysis of headlines has further applications. Suppose that a particular headline appears in gatherings A through D with a misprint and then in gatherings E through M with the misprint corrected. It would seem that gatherings A through D were composed, imposed, and printed before the others. Compositors working from manuscript generally set the preliminaries (title page, preface, etc.) after the rest of the book; since in this book the first gathering (A), containing the preliminaries, was evidently set before gatherings E–M, the book may well be a reprint of an earlier edition and not a direct descendant of a manuscript. Bibliographers may also infer the order of composition from headline variation, such as that seen in the progressive deterioration of or damage to type used in a headline or that caused by the failure to alter running titles to reflect changes in the contents of a book. And the presence of a headline unique to a particular leaf (or leaves) may indicate that the leaf is a cancel— that a leaf has been excised and replaced by another. Similarly, a whole gathering with headlines unrepeated in any other may be a cancel, the work of another compositor, or a sheet from an earlier edition. These inferences from headline analysis are often tentative, but they can be strengthened by corroborative evidence from paper, typography, compositorial habits, and other sources.

Because of its painstaking use of bibliographical analysis, Charlton Hinman's *The Printing and Proof-Reading of the First Folio of Shakespeare* (Oxford: Clarendon, 1963) can serve as a textbook in method. Studies of the Folio have been of two kinds. One, largely textual though employing bibliography, seeks to identify the setting copy used for each of the thirty-six plays, whether it is good quarto, bad quarto, corrected quarto, scribal fair copy, Shakespeare's foul papers, or some combination of these. The other is more strictly bibliographical, attempting to enter the printing shop of Issac Jaggard to observe the processes that produced the book. This kind of study also has textual applications, of course, for it may reveal the nature and extent of modifications the copy received during printing.

Hinman addressed himself to this second kind of study. Using a device of his own design (the Hinman collator), he compared multiple copies of the Folio and uncovered a great body of useful evidence, consisting mostly of textual variants and identifiable, recurrent pieces of type. Joined with other evidence and with reasonable assumptions about printing-shop practices, the results of his machine collation became the basis for conclusions about the number of copies printed, the number of presses used, the number of compositors and the parts set by each, the order in which parts were set, the type cases used by each compositor, the time taken in printing, the delays in printing, and the way the book was proofread and corrected. If Hinman did not get through the door of Jaggard's shop, he certainly achieved a good view from a window.

A central finding of Hinman's was that Jaggard set the book by formes rather than by successive pages. The Folio is so called because of its imposition format: pages of type were arranged so that each printed sheet was folded once to create two leaves, a total of four pages. Beyond that, the 1623 folio is in sixes—that is, each gathering consists of three quired folio sheets:

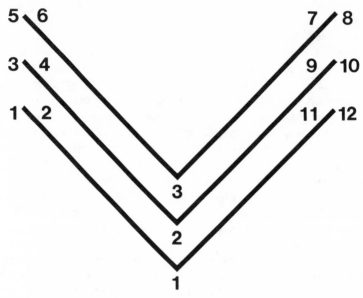

Fig. 2.   Folio in sixes. Three sheets are folded and quired to form a gathering of six leaves, or twelve pages.

One might expect that the compositors would begin setting type with the first page and then progress to the twelfth; they did not. Hinman identified about six hundred pieces of damaged type that recurred in the Folio, some over one hundred times. He found certain pieces not only in various six-leaf gatherings but also within one gathering, even within the first seven pages of a gathering. If a type appears on, say, page 1 and then again on page 5 of the same gathering, then the pages of the gathering could not have been set successively. For page 1 would be printed with page 12, its pair in the outer forme of the sheet. The type would then have to be returned to the case (i.e., distributed) before it could be used for setting and printing page 5. Thus, Hinman concluded, the Folio was set by formes. Page 1 was not set before page 5, though. Since a particular piece of type cannot occur in two consecutive formes (one being on the press while the other was being set), the pattern of recurrence indicated that most of the gatherings were set from the inside out: the inner forme of sheet 3 (pp. 6, 7), then the outer (pp. 5, 8), then the inner forme of sheet 2 (pp. 4, 9), and so on to the outer forme of sheet 1 (pp. 1, 12). Needless to say, this procedure required some calculation if the text were to fit into the pages. Faulty casting off, as the calculations are called, could result in either too much or too little text for the space available—a problem solved in some instances by altering the text.

Although Hinman's identification of the Folio's compositors and the portions set by each has been subject to argument and revision, his method is exemplary. He identified five compositors. The two who set most of the Folio were Compositor A (who preferred the spellings *doe*, *goe*, and *here*) and Compositor B (who preferred *do*, *go*, *heere*). Combining spelling evidence with that of types revealed that three type cases (each actually a complex of four cases) were used and that the cases could be assigned to compositors— for example, Case Y to Compositor B. Thus when spelling alone did not identify the compositor of a particular forme, the case might. If we know which compositor set what and if we know the habits of the compositors (e.g., that Compositor B made more errors than A and "took frequent and various liberties with his copy" [p. 10]), then we can better recover what Shakespeare actually wrote. What might appear to be an authorial alteration may in fact be a compositor's characteristic and perhaps ingenious misreading.

Hinman also found hundreds of textual variants that resulted from proof corrections (which occurred simultaneously with the printing). For two formes the press was stopped three times for correction. Most proofreading, he discovered, was "confined to some six or eight plays of one section" and largely to the work of one compositor, E, who may have been an apprentice (p. 227). Moreover, the proofing, generally late and careless, was concerned more with typographical appearance than with accuracy of text. The corrector, who may have been Jaggard himself, sometimes consulted copy, sometimes not.

Hinman did not discuss at any length the implications of his findings for literary study. But no editor or critic of Shakespeare can ignore them, nor can any student of analytical or historical bibliography. At the heart of his method was the discovery of a pattern of physical evidence that accorded with other patterns, with what is known about seventeenth-century printing, and with what can reasonably be assumed. Some of his conclusions are quite certain, others merely probable. Some already have been modified or challenged in the light of further evidence. Bibliographical knowledge is cumulative; if it begins by dropping chemical solutions on paper or by following a broken piece of type through hundreds of pages, it can end in significant conclusions. As Thoreau advised, "Let us not underrate the value of a fact; it will one day flower in a truth."

Hinman analyzed only one edition, but many of his methods, as well as those discussed earlier, can also be used in identifying and organizing the multiple editions and other forms that constitute a printing history. Again, the aim may be textual: to discover the relations between a text and its physical embodiments. It may be literary historical: to investigate, for example, the popularity of a work by determining the number of its editions. It may be bibliophilic: to aid the collector in acquiring all forms of a book. Or it may be purely bibliographical: to provide a basis of organization for a descriptive bibliography. Regardless of aim, the problem is to determine what the forms of a book are and how they are related. This task requires analytical bibliography, since the concepts used—edition, impression, state, and issue—are defined according to printing processes and are detectable through examination of physical evidence.

An edition, in the strict bibliographical sense, consists of all copies of a book that are printed from one setting of type, whether directly from the type or indirectly through plates made from it. (Modern phototypesetting creates an image without actually setting any metal type. All copies that reproduce the same image, though it may be photographically enlarged or reduced, belong to the same edition.) The act of typesetting, then, defines an edition. Revising the type does not create a new edition unless it is so extensive as to result in a substantially new setting. Identifying different editions, then, requires the detection of different settings of type. Thus alterations in typefaces, type size, and distribution of text on the pages are evidence of a new edition. Even when one edition is a line-for-line resetting of another, it will contain variations, at least in spacing of letters and words. Within an edition there may be several impressions (or printings), each consisting of all copies of an edition that are printed at any one time. Often, detecting different impressions is difficult, since the type may be unchanged. But if the set type has been considerably revised, one is probably dealing with a new impression. A new impression may be printed on a stock of paper different from that of another impression (different in watermark, distance between chain lines, thickness, color, ingredients, etc.), but this evidence is suggestive rather than conclusive, since two or more stocks may be used within a single impression. If, however, the first impression was known to be printed in 1850 and if some copies of the book are found with paper dated after that, then those copies obviously belong to another impression. A change in scheme of imposition is also evidence of a new impression. One impression may have its pages imposed to form gatherings of eight leaves, while another has its pages arranged for gatherings of sixteen. Even without such a change in imposition, there are likely to be measurable differences in the impositions of two impressions, especially in the "gutter" margins (the sum of the inner margins of two conjugate pages).

Until the development of stereotype plating in the early nineteenth century, editions generally consisted of but one impression. (Type for most books was too scarce and expensive to be kept standing; if, after printing one impression, publishers needed more copies of a book, type would have to be set again.) Plating is often detectable. Plates cast in plaster, for example, produce a type page slightly smaller than the type itself, since both the molds and the metal cast in them tend to shrink,[15] and twentieth-century photo-offset plates may reduce or enlarge the type-page image photographically. Distinguishing between multiple impressions printed from one set of plates requires the same evidence as distinguishing between impressions printed from type. And because plates, like type, were subject to damage and because the greatest damage would occur in handling and storage between impressions, the presence of damage also suggests a new impression, as does resetting to repair the damage.

Within an impression there may be two or more states. These may result from alterations in the type or plates during the printing of an impression, often through stop-press corrections. Or they may result later from a number of other causes, such as the insertion of an errata slip or the removal, or cancellation, of a page (which may be replaced by another). Often it is more accurate to assign states to sheets or even formes, since a particular copy of an impression may contain any of several combinations of corrected or uncorrected parts. An impression may also consist of more than one issue, an issue being all copies of an impression that are identifiable as a separate unit of sale. Unit of sale, of course, implies publishing rather than printing history, but for such a unit to be identifiable, it must contain some physical feature derived from its production. Often this feature is a variant title page, listing perhaps a different publisher or date, or it may be a cheaper or more expensive paper. Sometimes publishers take a certain number of copies of an impression, insert an extra page stating that the book is a "limited edition" and bearing the author's signature, and then sell these copies to collectors. Thus they create two issues—a limited issue and a trade issue—of one impression. The distinction between states and issues is that between mere variation and variation that signals a different unit of sale.

Our taxonomy of editions, impressions, issues, and states reflects printing and publishing history only if we also know the chronological sequence of these forms. A time-honored rule for determining the order of editions is that the handsomest is the first. The first edition establishes the reputation of the book. Subsequent editions can rely on that reputation rather than on appearance to gain buyers, and less handsome and therefore cheaper editions will appeal to another sector of the market. Thus today an edition bound in cloth and enclosed in a colorful jacket generally precedes the cheaper, smaller paperback edition. So too in, say, the seventeenth century the first edition might have been printed in a large format (e.g., folio), while later editions might have appeared in quarto, octavo, or sixteenmo. The first might have a two-color title page and blank pages between textual divisions, while later editions would have one-color title pages and few blank pages.

The care taken over the appearance of the first edition tends also to extend to the composition and printing. Later editions often have more misprints, and thus textual readings can aid in the determination of sequence. The kind of misprints may also be significant. R. B. McKerrow's *Introduction to Bibliography for Literary Students* (Oxford: Clarendon, 1928), still a good introduction to analytical bibliography, presents an example from Nashe's *Pierce Penilesse*, three editions of which were published in 1592.

Edition A: 'frantick'
Edition B: 'fran- / tick'
Edition C: 'fran-tick' (p. 196)

Edition A, known on other evidence to be first, prints the word midway in a line. It was followed by edition B, which broke the word between two lines. The compositor of edition C evidently used edition B as copy, setting the word midway in a line but incorrectly retaining the hypen.

Caution is required, however, in analyzing textual variants to determine the order of editions. Bibliographical taxonomy does not necessarily coincide with the textual stemma. The compositor or compositors setting type for a second edition cannot use a third edition for their copy, but they may not use the first edition either; they could use the same manuscript that served as a copy for the first edition. Likewise, a fifth edition may be set from any of four previous editions, from several editions, or from various manuscripts.

Naturally, a compositor would prefer to set from printed matter rather than from manuscript. Especially in the handpress period, it is sometimes possible to determine whether a book has been set from manuscript or is a "reprint" (not to be confused with reimpression) of a previously printed book. Again, McKerrow provides some general rules. Setting from a manuscript, a compositor generally began with the text itself rather than with the preliminaries (title page, preface, and the like), and thus would begin setting the second gathering of the book. Whether the compositor began with the text or with the preliminaries can sometimes be inferred from the way the book is "signed"—that is, from the sequence of letters, numbers, or other symbols that the compositor placed at the foot of the initial leaves of gatherings to ensure their proper arrangement in binding. If an edition has signatures "all of one alphabet, beginning with A and proceeding regularly," according to McKerrow, it is "likely to be later than an edition in which the preliminary leaves have a separate signature" (p. 190). Likewise, if the text of an edition starts on a leaf other than the first of a gathering, the edition is likely a reprint, for the compositor probably began setting with the preliminaries. A somewhat different application of McKerrow's observations can be made to these two editions of a book:

Edition X. Consists of 18 gatherings, each with 4 leaves. The first gathering is signed A, the second, a, the rest B through S. The preliminaries end on leaf a4 (the fourth leaf of the gathering signed a); the text begins on leaf B1.

Edition Y. It too consists of 18 gatherings of 4 leaves each. The first gathering is signed A, the second, B, and the rest, C through T. The text begins on leaf C1. (adapted from McKerrow, p. 190)

Edition X may well have been set from manuscript. The compositor perhaps began setting the text with gathering B, leaving A for the preliminaries, which turned out to be longer than expected and so required the additional gathering a. Edition Y is likely a reprint; otherwise, the compositor may not have known that the text would begin in gathering C. Such conclusions can often be supported by further evidence. Suppose, for example, that in edition Y the second leaf of gathering E bears the incorrect signature D2 and that editions X and Y contain, page for page, the same distribution of printed matter. It is likely that, forgetting the new system of signatures (which eliminated the minuscule a signature), the compositor missigned the leaf while reprinting edition Y from edition X.

General rules have specific exceptions and must be used cautiously. They are not substitutes for thorough bibliographical analysis. It might appear, for example, that the 1594 quarto of Christopher Marlowe's *Edward II* is a reprint of a now lost edition. It has a collation formula of A–M^4 (twelve gatherings of four leaves each), with the text beginning on leaf A2. But, as Fredson Bowers has shown, it probably is an original edition, set from manuscript rather than from any earlier edition.[16] Although the text begins in sheet A, setting began in sheet B. Thus, as was usual with editions set from manuscript, the preliminaries were set last. One bit of evidence for this conclusion comes from the skeleton formes. Through the distinctive appearance of running titles, Bowers identified two skeleton formes in this quarto, one skeleton used for the inner forme of every sheet (the side containing pages 2, 3, 6, and 7) and the other for the outer forme. But a peculiar dislocation of the running titles in sheet A suggests that A was printed after M, since the dislocation resulted from three blank pages in sheet M. This evidence coincides with the pattern of recurrence of identifiable pieces of type. Types distributed from sheet B reappear in sheet D, types from C reappear in E, and so on to the end; then types from L reappear in A; but no sheet seems to have been set from distributed types of sheet A. Thus the preliminaries and the text of sheet A were set last. Further corroboration comes from the text and depends on the identification of the compositors. There were two. In addition to having different spelling habits, they differed in their practice of using signatures. Compositor X regularly supplied signatures for the first three leaves of his sheets (sigs. A–E), and compositor Y regularly supplied them for the first two leaves of his (sigs. F–M). This information can then be applied to the question of whether the quarto is a reprint. There is considerable disparity between the two compositors' abilities to lineate the verse of Marlowe's play, compositor Y mislining much more frequently than X. If the 1594 quarto were a reprint, the compositors would probably have followed the earlier edition's lineation and thus would not have produced the disparity (except in the unlikely event that the prior edition also had two compositors who set the same shares as X and Y did in 1594). On the basis of this bibliographical evidence, Bowers concludes that the 1594 quarto is a first edition set from manuscript and not a reprint of a lost earlier edition.

In recovering the sequence in which several editions were printed, the bibliographer can also use the evidence provided by progressive deterioration, or batter, of type and ornaments (just as Hinman used type batter within Shakespeare's First Folio to determine the order in which its parts were printed). A woodcut ornament, for example, may be in pristine condition in a first edition, slightly damaged in a second, and greatly damaged in a third. Such damage may also serve to date an edition, if the dates of other books using the ornament are known and if there is a clear progression of deterioration. Similarly, the progressive batter (and repair) of plates may both differentiate impressions and establish their sequence.

This sort of evidence from analytical bibliography, corroborated with publisher's records and other secondary evidence, reveals the history of the three 1850 editions of *The Scarlet Letter* published by Ticknor and Fields.[17] The first edition consists of one impression, printed from type. It exists in two states, because gathering 21 was set in duplicate, presumably for more economical handling of this short final gathering. After the type for all gatherings through 13 and for part of gatherings 14 and 15 had been distributed, the publisher required additional copies of the novel. Resetting the portion already distributed and joining it with the undistributed type from gatherings 14 through 21, the printer manufactured more copies—a second edition, since the type was substantially reset. After the printing of these copies, the second-edition type was distributed. Later the same year, still more copies were wanted. Again type was set, creating a third edition, but this time stereotype plates were made from the type. One impression was printed from the plates in 1850 (followed by many more over the following years).

Bibliographically, it is not an especially remarkable or complex history. Yet it was unavailable until discovered by the bibliographical analysis undertaken for the Centenary Hawthorne. Textual critics have benefited from the demonstration that resetting and thus opportunities for textual variation occurred. There are sixty-nine variant readings between the first and second editions, for example. Literary historians now have some indication that, whatever enthusiasm James T. Fields may have expressed for the novel as a literary work, he must have harbored doubts about its prospective sales; otherwise he would have had plates made right from the start and would not have waited until the third setting of the type.[18] Collectors will be interested to know that the variously dated advertisements bound with the first-edition copies do not reflect the dates of the sheets. In short, all those who study materials transmitted through the medium of print can use the findings of analytical bibliography, even if only indirectly through its applications in descriptive bibliography and textual criticism.

3.

Descriptive Bibliography

A conventional entry in an enumerative bibliography looks like this:

Styron, William. *The Confessions of Nat Turner.*
New York: Random House, 1967.

The entry makes no distinction between the first impression, the second impression (the text of which differs from that of the first in twelve readings), the third impression (with two more variant readings), the fourth impression (with twelve more), and the fifth (with another twelve).[19] It could refer to any or all. Scholars, however, need a more precise record of the forms in which the novel has been presented to the public. Such a history of books as books is called a descriptive bibliography and has a number of purposes that justify its presentation and determine its methods: (1) to give a thorough account of a group of books (and other printed forms, such as periodicals) to help textual and literary critics locate those containing the texts that are their subjects of study, (2) to serve as a source of identification, a standard against which a particular copy of a book can be compared, (3) to organize the books according to bibliographical taxonomy and to present the evidence on which the findings are based, and (4) to contribute to the larger history of printing and publishing by investigating a portion of it.

If identification were the only purpose, much of the detail found in descriptive bibliographies could be dispensed with. Often, a few points will serve to differentiate the various editions, impressions, issues, and states. The presence of these points (a misprint, a particular watermark, the position of a signature, etc.) in the copy at hand would identify the book. But this assumes that the bibliographer has managed to examine and record every possible form of the book. Even if the bibliographer has been successful, the result is little more than a guide for collectors. It is not descriptive bibliography, for it does not provide a printing and publishing history of use to literary critics and historians, textual critics, and bibliographers themselves. In a descriptive bibliography one could learn, for example, that the second edition of Louis Un-

27

termeyer's *Modern American Poetry* (1921) appeared in a size and in a grayish-green binding that make it seem, in looks as well as in contents, an imitation of *The New Poetry* (1917), a successful anthology edited by Harriet Monroe and Alice Corbin Henderson. Similarly, a descriptive bibliography would show that the first English impression of Styron's *The Confessions of Nat Turner* was printed from offset plates that were made by combining pages of two Random House impressions, thereby producing a bastard impression with both early and late stages of the text (which was further complicated by the English publisher's introducing other textual variants). And such a bibliography would demonstrate, by identifying five different types used in the running titles, that Dekker's *Magnificent Entertainment* (1604), a quarto of thirty-six leaves, was evidently printed in five sections by as many different presses.

The kinds and amount of detail presented in a descriptive bibliography are determined, then, by its multiple purposes and by the materials dealt with. In general, whatever physical features may be useful in analytical bibliography are those given most attention in descriptive bibliography, both as evidence for the conclusions presented and as material for further analysis. Thus one finds collation formulas, records of running titles, and descriptions of paper and typography, for example.

How descriptions should be accommodated to the materials has been a matter of controversy, focused in discussions of the "degressive principle." This phrase was used by Falconer Madan, who was writing before the flowering of the New Bibliography.[20] He meant by it that description should vary according to the period or importance of the books being treated. The principle is sound, the application difficult. For Madan it meant that incunables (books printed before 1501) required detailed descriptions and modern books almost none. In author bibliographies, the principle has been used as a rationale for limiting the treatment given editions appearing after the author's lifetime or containing nonauthoritative texts, though this practice has been criticized for neglecting printing and publishing history. Not controversial, though, is the principle that the kind of detail must vary with changes in the production processes. In modern printing, for example, there has been an increased standardization and uniformity of product. Minute differences—often all that distinguish multiple impressions—may be detected by machine collation (using the Hinman collator or Lindstrand comparator), measurements of gutter margins, or other forms of analysis, and thus definitive descriptions of these books must include such detail. So too must the specificity of detail suit the objects described. Since variations of one to three millimeters in type-page size may indicate plating in nineteenth-century books, it does no good to report their measurements merely to the nearest centimeter. The degree of specificity, however, must not be so high as to make every copy of a book (or every sheet or forme) a variant state. In bibliographical taxonomy as in biological, there are the "lumpers" and "splitters." Where lumpers may see one state, splitters may see four. Yet both agree that descriptions should give the range of variation and that states should be significant points within the range—significant in that they reflect alterations (intended or not) in the methods, materials, or circumstances of printing. Every copy of an edition is unique in some way, however slight, but descriptive bibliographers do not describe particular copies: they describe the editions, impressions, issues, and states, after examining as many particular copies as feasible. In doing so, they describe what is sometimes called "ideal copy," which has been defined thus by G. Thomas Tanselle:

> The *standard or "ideal"* copy ... is a historical reconstruction of the form or forms of the copies of an impression or issue as they were released to the public by their producer. Such a reconstruction thus encompasses all states of an impression or issue, whether they result from design or accident; and it excludes alterations that occurred in individual copies after the time when those copies ceased to be under the control of the printer or publisher.[21]

A full bibliographical description answers seven questions that more or less correspond to the divisions within it: (1) What is the book—what edition, for example? This question is answered in the heading of the description. (2) What does the book say about itself in the title page, colophon, copyright page, and other imprints? (3) How was the book put together? Considered here are the imposition format, collation formula, and pagination. (4) What does the book contain? (5) What is the book made of? What sort of type and paper were used? (6) How was the book packaged in a binding and dust jacket? (7) What is known, from bibliographical analysis and other sources, about the printing and publishing of the book, its variant states, and the irregularities of particular copies?

The descriptive methods that answer these questions have been standardized in Fredson Bowers' *Principles of Bibliographical Description* (1949; rpt. New York: Russell, 1962). There have also been recent elaborations and refinements, notably in a number of articles by G. Thomas Tanselle (listed in the reference bibliography). Because various bibliographers may prefer modifications to suit their materials or fancy, users of descriptive bibliographies should consult whatever introductory and explanatory matter these works contain. Our purpose here, as we consider each of these questions, is to furnish not instruction in how to describe books but rather an introduction to some of the methods for those who may use descriptive bibliographies and for those who want an overview before reading further in the area.

WHAT IS THE BOOK?

Each entry in a descriptive bibliography begins with a heading that identifies the item and assigns it a number that indicates its position in the bibliography and serves as a means of precise reference in book catalogs, scholarly studies, and the bibliography itself. A typical author bibliography consists of several lettered sections within which chronology and bibliographical taxonomy serve as the bases of organization. The number and identifying nomenclature reflect that organization. Thus section A (separately published works) of C. E. Frazer Clark's Hawthorne bibliography gives the following headings for some entries described under A16, Hawthorne's sixteenth book:

A 16	THE SCARLET LETTER
A 16.1	First edition, only printing 1850
A 16.2	Second edition, only printing 1850
A 16.3.a	Third edition, first printing (first plated edition) 1850
A 16.3.b	Third edition, second printing 1851
A 16.3.c	Third edition, third printing 1851

. . . .

A 16.13.a1	Riverside Edition (trade), first printing, American issue 1883
A 16.13.a2	Riverside Edition (trade), first printing, English issue 1883
A 16.13.b	Riverside edition (large paper), second printing 1883[22]

WHAT DOES THE BOOK SAY ABOUT ITSELF?

Title pages, copyright pages, and colophons present information, sometimes inaccurate, about authors, titles, places of publication, publishers, printers, and so forth. In both the information conveyed and the typographical means of conveying it, these parts of books often serve as identification. The title page can also be viewed as the book's public face, which, through the arrangement, selection, and emphasis of its features, can imply how the book was to meet and court its potential readers. In design and wording, for example, early title pages of Swift's *Travels into Several Remote Nations of the World*, commonly known as *Gulliver's Travels*, closely resembled those of authentic travel narratives enjoying great popularity in the early eighteenth century. For these reasons, title pages are often photographically reproduced or rendered in quasi facsimile.

Quasi-facsimile transcription attempts to give a sense of the title page or other matter without reproducing it photographically. It transcribes the precise wording, including spelling, punctuation, and capitalization (though large and small capitals are differentiated only if they occur in the same line); reduces styles of type to three (roman, *italic,* and 𝔟𝔩𝔞𝔠𝔨 𝔩𝔢𝔱𝔱𝔢𝔯); and indicates line endings with a vertical stroke (ignoring variations in the spacing of lines). Especially in pre-eighteenth-century books, certain typographical features cause difficulty, in part because modern type fonts do not contain some types that were then common. Thus some bibliographies ignore the distinction between long s (f) and short s and do not reproduce ligatures (such as ff and ct), though the digraphs æ and œ are usually reproduced. Swash (or scriptlike) letters, especially swash italic capitals *J* and *V,* are usually indicated, as are tailed italic letters ($\smile$, m, n). Even if lacking in modern fonts, such typographical features can be recorded by bracketed comments within the transcription, by description following it, or by special symbols (a tailed *m,* for example, may be indicated as *m*[.]). Within a transcription, the printing is assumed to be black unless otherwise noted. Such features as ornaments, rules, drawings, and devices are noted or described. Many title pages are enclosed in borders—either compartments (enclosures of single design and made up of an engraving or wood-cut to form a single piece, even if later cut into more than one) or frames (enclosures of separate type ornaments, wood-cuts, or rules pieced together). These borders are described and, if possible, identified in such standard references as R. B. McKerrow and F. S. Ferguson's *Title-Page Borders Used in England and Scotland, 1485–1640* (London: Bibliographical Soc., 1932). Whenever transcriptions cannot reproduce a required item, it is described in square brackets. These descriptions will vary according to the level of accuracy used in the bibliographies. One might describe a rule merely as '[rule],' while another might write '[short rule]' and yet another write '[rule, 21 mm.].' (Note that quotations of quasi facsimile are enclosed in single quotation marks to distinguish them from ordinary quotations.) Figure 4 shows Fredson Bowers' transcription of the title page in figure 3:

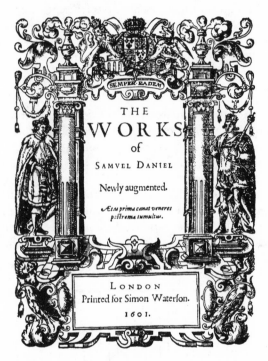

Fig. 3.   Title page.

[within a sected compartment: McK. & F. 229] THE | WORKS | of | SᴀᴍᴠᴇL Dᴀɴɪᴇʟ | Newly augmented. | *Ætas prima canat veneres* | *postrema tumultus.* | [within a slot] Lᴏɴᴅᴏɴ | Printed for Simon Waterfon. | 1601.   [WORKS *with* W *from filed* VV, *the first with shortened limb*]

Fig. 4.   Quasi-facsimile transcription of title page in fig. 3.

Had a portion of the title page been in a color other than black, that fact would be noted within brackets:

THE | [red] WORKS | of | SAMVEL DANIEL|
[black] Newly augmented.   [...]

The color indicator applies to all items that follow it until a change is noted; in the example, the second, third, and fourth lines are in red. (An alternative is to begin the transcription with the notation '[in black and <u>red</u>]' and then underscore the red portions.) Bibliographers sometimes indicate colors more precisely by including a reference to the numbered color samples in the National Bureau of Standards' centroid color charts: '[dark red, centroid 16].'

The same techniques of quasi-facsimile transcription are applied to colophons (notes located at the ends of books and giving information about their printing and publishing) and to any other items, such as those on the copyright pages of modern books, that give similar information.

HOW WAS THE BOOK PUT TOGETHER?

This question is answered principally by a formula of format and collation, which reflects how pages of type were arranged for printing sheets of paper and how, after printing, these sheets were folded to make leaves and arranged within the book. During the handpress period, the most common formats for the imposition of type pages were folio (2°), quarto (4°), octavo (8°), and duodecimo (12°).[23] If we recall what paper from this period looks like, it is clear that the direction of chain lines and position of the watermark are clues to imposition. As figure 5 shows, the chain lines of a folio run vertically on the leaves, and the watermark is centered in one leaf (the countermark, if any, in the other).

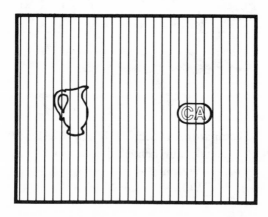

Fig. 5. Sheet of paper, with watermark on the left, countermark on the right, and vertical chain lines.

In a quarto the sheet is folded twice to make four leaves (eight pages), with the chain lines horizontal and the watermark in the middle of the spine fold (i.e., the gutter). In an octavo, the sheet is folded three times to produce eight leaves, with the chain lines vertical and the watermark at the head of the spine fold. For a duodecimo, also called twelvemo, the sheet can be folded (and perhaps cut) in several ways. In one (common 12°), it is folded twice across the longer dimension and thrice across the shorter, making twelve leaves; its chain lines will be horizontal, and the watermarks will appear toward the top of leaves 7 and 8 (or 11 and 12). In another (long 12°), the sheet is folded once across the short side and five times across the longer, making 12 leaves; its chain lines will be vertical, and the watermark will appear at the top of the outer margin of leaves 5 and 6 (or 11 and 12). In the machine-press period, imposition format is difficult or impossible to ascertain, because wove paper robs us of chain lines and because books are printed from multiple impositions on very large sheets or on rolls of paper. In descriptions of these books, therefore, the measurement of a typical leaf sometimes replaces the format notation in the formula.

From the example of Shakespeare's First Folio, it will be recalled that one sheet could be inserted (quired) into another after folding and before binding. Thus the Folio was a folio in sixes, each section (called a gathering) consisting of three folio sheets and thus six leaves. So too could a quarto sheet be quired with another to form a quarto in eights. Or, after a process called half-sheet imposition, a sixteen could be cut in half to form two gatherings of eight leaves each. In other words, the imposition format does not necessarily coincide with the scheme of gathering (though, of course, the type pages would have to be imposed so that their sequence would be correct after any quiring or cutting).

To aid binders in arranging the printed sheets (and to provide a means of reference when pagination or foliation was absent), compositors included marks called signatures toward the foot of the rectos (right-hand pages) of some leaves. A folio in sixes, for example, might have signatures on the rectos of leaves 1, 2, and 3 of each gathering. In England, the usual practice was and is to use as signatures the letters of the twenty-three-letter Latin alphabet (which omits *J, U,* and *W).* In American books, one may find the Latin alphabet, the twenty-six-letter alphabet, or numbers. The arrangement of sheets in gatherings can thus be expressed in a formula that uses the signatures to designate the gatherings and adds superscript figures to indicate the number of leaves in each gathering:

2°: A–H^6; 48 leaves.

Translated, this collation formula means that twenty-four folio sheets were arranged in eight gatherings (A–H), each gathering consisting of three sheets and thus six leaves and the whole book consisting of forty-eight leaves. If the signatures had been set in lowercase type or in numbers, these characters would replace the capitals:

$2°$: a–h^6; 48 leaves.
$2°$: 1–8^6; 48 leaves.

In books containing more than twenty-three gatherings and thus exhausting the alphabet, compositors usually began the alphabet anew with doubled letters (e.g., Aa or AA) and, if that group was exhausted, with tripled letters, and so on. A book with sixty-nine gatherings would thus have this formula:

$2°$: A–3Z^6; 414 leaves.

Within all examples so far, the gatherings have contained the same number of leaves. Often, however, there may be unequal gatherings:

$2°$: A^2 B–2E^4 2F–2G^2; 114 leaves.

It is also common to find books in which some gatherings are not signed. Often a signing can be inferred from the sequence and is indicated in square brackets:

$2°$: [A]^2 B–K^4 [L]^4 M–2E^4 2F^2 [2G]^2; 114 leaves.

If the unsigned gathering is preliminary and cannot be inferred, it is given as pi (π); if it appears elsewhere and cannot be inferred, it is given as chi (χ):

$2°$: π^2 A–G^4 χ^2 H–Z^4; 96 leaves.

The formula can even describe totally unsigned books or books in which the system of signing does not correspond to the actual folding. The bibliographer can identify the gatherings by knowing what sizes of gatherings are likely for the particular format and by locating the two conjugate leaves (and stitching) at the center of each gathering. In such a case the formula might look like this:

$4°$: [A]^2 [B–H]^4; 30 leaves.

The formula also takes account of leaves that have been added, removed, or removed and replaced by a cancel:

$4°$: A^8 ($-$A3) B–D^8 ($\pm$D7) E–F^8 (F6 + 1.2); 49 leaves.

In this example, leaf 3 of gathering A has been excised; leaf 7 of gathering D has been cancelled and a new leaf inserted in its place; and two conjugate leaves in gathering F have been added after leaf 6 (if the two added leaves were disjunct, a comma would replace the period, as in F6 + 1,2). The final item in the formula is a statement of where the signatures actually appear in each gathering:

4°: A–F⁴; 24 leaves; $3 signed.

The dollar sign is simply a convenient notation for all gatherings. The number that follows it indicates the leaves that bear signatures. In this example, then, the first three leaves of each gathering are signed. Any irregularities in signing are also noted:

4°: A–F⁴; 24 leaves; $3 signed (− A1, B3; + A4; F2 missigned 'G2').

The first three leaves in each gathering are signed, with the exception of leaves A1 and B3 and with the addition of leaf A4, and leaf F2 bears the wrong signature 'G2.'

Though not strictly part of the collation formula, a statement of pagination (or of foliation if leaves rather than pages are numbered) generally appears with it. Like the formula, this statement accounts for every leaf in the book. If every page were numbered, a pagination formula might look like this: pp. i–iv, 1–88. Often, however, some pages lack page numbers. If the numbers can be inferred, they are placed in square brackets; otherwise, the total number of adjacent numberless pages is reported by an italic figure in square brackets: pp. [*2*] i–ii, [*1–4*] 5–88. Misnumberings or misprintings of numbers are noted after the record of pagination.

Finally, for certain books, a record is made of press figures and catchwords. Press figures, in use from the late seventeenth through the early nineteenth centuries, appeared at the bottom of a page within a forme and marked that forme as the work of particular press or press operator. They are useful, therefore, in analyzing the presswork of a book; moreover, because the figures would be altered from impression to impression, they are useful for identification. How the figures are recorded varies from one bibliography to another, depending on what sort of chart, table, or list best exposes whatever pattern they make.[24] One method, not as revealing as a table, simply lists the figures and then the pages on which they appear:

1: A5r A7v C5r C7v
2: B3r B6r
3: D2v

Another procedure, recording the entries seriatim as page and figure (7–6, 14–2, etc.), quickly discloses any variation as one checks through the book, revealing at once, for example, three concealed impressions of Samuel Johnson's *The False Alarm*, "Second Edition," 1770.

Catchwords, in general use from the mid–sixteenth century through the eighteenth, helped printers arrange the type pages in the proper order for printing. (A catchword appears at the bottom of a page and anticipates the first word on the following page.) In addition to noting any miscatchings and absent catchwords, a bibliography may record all catchwords, a sample, or just those on the last page of each gathering.

WHAT DOES THE BOOK CONTAIN?

In addition to its obvious literary purpose, a list of a book's contents serves a bibliographical one. The arrangement of matter within the gatherings, as we saw in Chapter 2, may suggest whether the book is an original edition or a reprint. It also serves as a further means of identification. The list of contents accounts for every page, from first to last, including blank pages. References to pages of handpress books take the form of signature and leaf number plus the notations r and v (some bibliographers use a and b), which designate rectos (the fronts of leaves) and versos (the backs of leaves). References to pages of machine-press books generally use page numbers. The content of the pages is described, quoted (usually without quotation marks), or rendered in quasi facsimile (within single quotation marks). The contents of a book from the seventeenth century might be described as follows:

> π1r–v blank, followed by engraved title page; π2r printed title page; π2v blank; π3r dedication 'To | THE MOST NOBLE | *John Doe* | [rule, 5 mm.]'; π3v blank; π4r–v prefatory poem; A1–R4r text; R4v blank.

Because running titles label the sections of a book and thus can be an identifying feature and because in early books they may be evidence as to the setting of the formes, they are often recorded after the contents listing or elsewhere. For one method of recording them, see the sample description in figure 6.

WHAT IS THE BOOK MADE OF?

To answer this question, bibliographers describe the type and paper. A description of type (or, more accurately, its inked image) may include all or some of this information: the number of lines on a typical page, the size of the type page (height before width), the height of twenty (ten in modern books) lines of type, the type-face size and x height in millimeters, the actual point size of the type body and leading if it can be determined, and the style of type. Type style may be denoted with varying levels of specificity—as one of several large divisions (e.g., Renaissance, Baroque, Neo-Classical, Free Roman), as a group within these divisions (e.g., Early Renaissance, English Baroque, Modern Neo-Classical), as subgroup (in Late Renaissance, e.g., are Caslon, Garamond, etc.), or as a specific font identified in a specimen book (e.g., Lanstom Monotype 268). Note may also be made of such features as particular broken types, identifiable ornaments, the positions of page numbers, the use of rules to frame the text, and gutter-margin measurements. The description of paper may include the size of the sheets, size of leaves, color, kind of paper (laid or wove), direction of chain lines (horizontal or vertical), distance between chain lines, watermarks (their size, location, and description), thickness of a single leaf, and the thickness of all leaves taken together.

How Was the Book Packaged?

Before the 1820s, the binding of books generally had little or no connection with their printing and publishing. Retail booksellers would sell books that were unbound, that they themselves had bound, or that specialist bookbinders had bound for them. The bindings of this period, therefore, do not constitute part of ideal copy; like owners' bookplates or coffee stains, they are features of individual copies. This is not to say that bindings lack significance. They were products of an art and craft and are studied as such. They also are valuable clues to the provenance of the particular copies that they contain. But, except insofar as they are secondary evidence, the bindings of this period are not treated in descriptive bibliographies. In the 1820s, however, with the development of new materials and mechanization and of new marketing patterns, edition binding became common. Large numbers of copies were bound uniformly in prefabricated cases before delivery to booksellers. The binding thus became part of ideal copy. These bindings sometimes serve to identify separate editions or impressions, and as a sort of packaging they suggest how books were sold and the markets they were intended to reach. Still, the connection between binding and sheets, even after the 1820s, can be tenuous. Old sheets may appear in a late binding, for example, and books may even appear in wrong bindings.

For bibliographers, a binding consists of more than covers. It includes the endpapers—sheets folded once into two halves, one half being pasted to the inside of a cover and the other allowed to stand free as protection of the leaves of the book—and whatever blank leaves or advertisements were bound up with the book, if they are not integral to the printed sheets.

In describing a binding, bibliographers note first the cloth or other materials of its cover. Especially in the nineteenth century, a wide variety of patterns were embossed on binding cloth: ripples, waves, checkerboards, dots and lines, hexagons, and the like. If reference is made to a standard system of nomenclature and classification, these patterns may be described quite accurately, as can their colors by reference to the centroid color charts: "Diagonal wave-cloth (Tanselle 106ae), brownish black (centroid 65)." Next, in summary or quasi facsimile, is reported the printed, stamped, or blind-stamped matter on the front, spine, and back. Binding usually affects the actual sheets of the book; their edges may be sprinkled, gilded, strained, trimmed, cut, or left unopened. Endpapers, binder's leaves, and nonintegral advertisements are described both as material (i.e., as paper) and for whatever decoration or printed matter they may contain.

Dust jackets, in common use since the 1880s, are also described with the binding. Attention is given to the kind of paper and to the contents of the front, spine, back, and flaps. Aside from their strictly bibliographical significance, dust jackets are of interest because they often contain illustrations by important artists, include blurbs in which authors puff their own work, or print criticism by other authors who were asked for statements to promote the work

WHAT IS KNOWN ABOUT THE PRINTING AND PUBLISHING OF THE BOOK?

The bibliographical description ends with the binding and is followed by notes that often constitute a lengthy discussion of the book's history, as revealed by bibliographical analysis and secondary evidence. Among the topics deserving mention are the variant states of the book, the peculiarities of individual copies, the relation of the book's text to that of other editions, the number of copies printed, the identity of the printer and compositors, the precise date of publication, the prices at which copies were sold, the date of copyright, references to the book in contemporary advertisements and trade records (e.g., the *Stationers' Register, Term Catalogues, Publishers Weekly*), the contemporary reaction to the book in reviews and elsewhere, and the arrangements (financial and otherwise) between the author and publisher. Finally, the bibliographical entry lists the locations of the specific copies that were consulted in preparing the description.

TWO SAMPLE DESCRIPTIONS

The first example (fig. 6) is taken from W. W. Greg's *A Bibliography of the English Printed Drama to the Restoration*, II (London: Oxford Univ. Press, 1951), pp. 641–42. The description generally employs the methods we have outlined. A few of Greg's abbreviations and conventions may require explanation: "HT" refers to the half title; "SR" refers to the *Stationers' Register*; and the double vertical line after "1634" in the title-page transcription indicates a rule that extends entirely or almost entirely across the type page.

The second example (fig. 7) is provided by Matthew J. Bruccoli and Richard Layman's *Ring W. Lardner: A Descriptive Bibliography* (Pittsburgh: Univ. of Pittsburgh Press, 1976), pp. 45–48. The description uses photographic reproductions rather than quasi-facsimile transcriptions for title and copyright pages. The parenthetical numbers in the description of the binding refer to the color samples in the centroid color charts. The measurement following the description of type records the height times the width of the type page, with the parenthetical number indicating the height of the type page plus the running titles.

In addition to such descriptions of books, a typical descriptive bibliography contains descriptions or at least lists of all other relevant forms of publication for its subject: periodicals, recordings, motion pictures, musical scores, drawings, and so forth. Descriptive bibliographies devoted to individual authors may also list manuscripts of their works and may include a reference list of works about the authors, though these are not, strictly speaking, matters of descriptive bibliography.

As histories of the physical forms in which texts have met the public, descriptive bibliographies are an essential means of access to the raw materials of literary study. To assume that these texts remain stable as they pass from one form to another would be naive indeed. As the next chapter shows, texts change.

497 The Temple of Love   (10 Feb.–24 Mar. 1635) 1634

(*a***) THE | TEMPLE | *OF* | LOVE. | A Mafque. | Prefented by the Qveenes Ma-|jefty,
1634 and her Ladies, at *White-hall* on | Shrove-Tuefday, 1634. ‖ By *Inigo Iones*,
Surveyour of his Majefties | Workes; and *William Davenant*, her Ma-|jefties
Servant. | [double rule] | *LONDON:* | Printed for *Thomas Walkley*, and are to
be fold at his | Shop neare *White-hall*. 1634.   [*OF* (*F* possibly a broken *E*)]
    †)   *variant title*] [as above except] By *Inigo Iones*, Surveyor of his Maties. Workes, |
and *William Davenant*, her Maties. Servant. [&c. as above]
          HT] THE TEMPLE | OF LOVE.
          RT] *The Temple of Love*. [semi-colon on C4^v]
Collation: 4°,   A⁴ B⁴(−B4) C⁴ D²,   13 leaves unnumbered.
Title, A1 (verso blank). 'The Argument', A2. Text with HT, A3. 'The Masquers Names'
(headed by 'The Queenes Majesty') and those of 'The Lords and others that presented the Noble
Persian Youths' on D2 (verso blank).
Catchwords: A–B, D. Poefie.   B3–C, 3. *and* [B4^v, Barque,]   C–D, Thelema.   *FꝪ NꝪS.*
The speeches are in verse, with prose argument.
Notes—1. The type of the title was altered in the course of printing, and the abnormally wide space
    above the double rule in (*a*⁺) shows this to be the later. The object of the change was apparently to
    give greater prominence to Davenant's name, which in the original setting was in smaller type
    than Jones's.
    2. The leaf B4 was evidently meant to be cancelled though it appears to be present in the majority
    of copies. The sheet had already been printed off when it was discovered that the entry of a Persian
    Page had been omitted on B4. The composition of sheet C was therefore begun so as to connect
    with B3^v and the matter originally filling the two pages of B4 was reset with the addition and
    a slight consequential alteration.
    3. The performance was on 10 Feb. 1635, and the dates on the title therefore follow the legal
    reckoning.
Copies: (*a***)   BM (C. 34. i. 37, +B4)   Bodl. (D2 def., +B4)   Wise   Boston   Hunt.
    Yale
    (*a*⁺)   BM (1073. i. 5/4, wants B1)   Dyce (+B4)   Chapin   Folger   Hunt.

SR 1658 Mar. 6.   *Tr. T. Walkley to H. Moseley: The Temple of Love, a Masque at Whitehall
    on Shrove Tuesday 1634, by Sir William Davenant.*

Adv. 1660. 'The Temple of Love, a Masque at White-Hall on Shrove-Tuesday, 1634. by Sir
    W. Davenant, Knight' is advertised among 'Comedies and Tragedies' 'Printed for Humphrey
    Moseley' as no. 242 in his separate List VI^B.

SR 1667 Aug. 19 (*see* Collection).   *Temple of Love.*

Fig. 6.   W. W. Greg's description of The Temple of Love *(1634).*

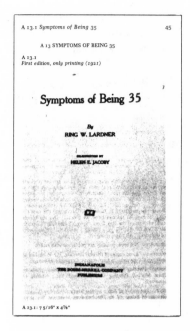

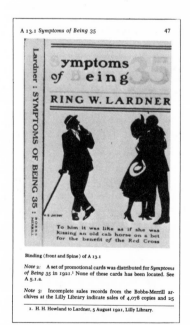

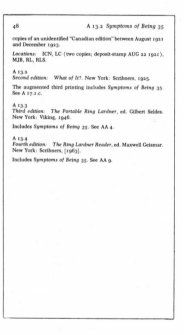

Fig. 7.   Bruccoli and Layman's description of Ring Lardner's Symptoms of Being 35 *(1921).*

4.

A Text and Its Embodiments

As we said earlier, the text is primary to literary studies. To make more concrete an understanding of how a text passes through its various embodiments, we would like to trace a complete history of two imaginary texts, one produced during the handpress period (1455–1800) and the other during the machine-press period (1801–   ). We constructed these examples to illustrate as many features as possible of the transmission of texts in each period; few actual texts would have survived in all these forms, and not every actual text would have passed through all these stages, whether they had been preserved down to our time or not.

THE LIFE OF A TEXT FROM THE HANDPRESS PERIOD

Of course, any text begins life in the mind of the author. Fortunately, or unfortunately, this form of the text is never available for study. However, letters, diaries, commonplace books, and similar documents may give some indication of ideas the author had before he set pen to paper (e.g., Milton's list of possible subjects in the Trinity manuscript). Only in rare instances will this form of the text, if indeed it is one, be of great use to the textual critic. After the idea for the work come notes of various sorts, from a rough outline of the entire work to rather full drafts of portions. Let us suppose that from these notes our hypothetical author attempts the first rough-draft manuscript (Rd 1). It is unlikely that he will get it just the way he wants it with the first effort, so he will probably produce a series of autograph manuscripts, each bearing successive alterations in the text (Rd 2–4). Were all these manuscripts to survive, we would see how the work evolved from its earliest rough form to something like the state the author desired.

Now several things might happen, but let us use a complex example. The author makes one fair copy in his own hand for his own use (Fc 1). From this copy he then produces, again in his own hand, another fair copy for presentation to a patron (Fc 2) and yet another fair copy to show to his colleagues for their judgment (Fc 3). (These people in turn might make additional copies.) Thus, at this stage we have three autograph fair-copy manuscripts by the author, but like most writers, as he makes each successive fair copy he alters the text. Although all three manuscripts are written by the author, each presents a slightly different version of the text. However, two manuscripts (Fc 2 and Fc 3) derive from the copy he keeps for himself, and it, in turn, derives from his working drafts. Although the first sets of notes and rough drafts were successive, the author later goes back and consults them and conflates his text as the work approaches maturity. Rough draft 3 is almost "it" but not quite; rough draft 4 is produced by consulting all previous drafts; and the first fair copy substantially duplicates rough draft 4 but also adds some things from rough draft 3.

Although his patron would probably not suggest any revisions, it is likely that his colleagues would do so, even marking on the manuscript circulated among them, and that the author would accept some of their suggestions while rejecting others. He might even revise his personal copy so as to adopt the suggestions he prefers.

The author might then think the work sufficiently advanced to employ a professional copyist to prepare a much more elaborate and careful copy, or several copies, for circulation to friends and possible patrons. This scribal copy (Sc) derives from the personal fair copy but conflates it with at least the fair copy sent to colleagues and includes alterations made, purposely or not, by the scribe or scribes.

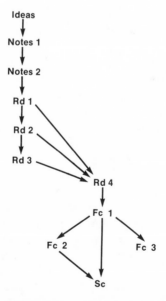

Fig. 8.   Textual transmission, from ideas to scribal copy.

By this time the author has sought or attracted the interest of a printer-publisher. Although the range of copies that an author might supply to a publisher is almost limitless, in our hypothetical instance the author uses the scribal copy, with some minor revisions made in his own hand. From this the printer begins to prepare the work for printing. First, the printer-publisher decides on the size of the edition to be printed, the typography, the format, and other such technical matters. (Until the eighteenth century authors usually had little say about any step in the publication process.) The printer then decides whether to print the book by formes or seriatim, depending on the number of compositors employed, the amount of work under way, and the time allotted for production. To print by formes the printer must cast off the manuscript—that is, mark it into units closely approximating a type page in this particular typography—and pass it on to the compositors for setting. We currently do not know how much a master printer, or the printer's staff, might tinker with the text of the manuscript before giving it to the compositors. But we do know that the compositors, simply by making another copy of the work, would introduce variations into the text, by either accident or design, just as the author had done when he produced Fc 2 and Fc 3 or as the copyist had done when producing Sc.

Sometime between the completion of composition and the ending of the pressrun, a member of the printing-house staff might look over printed sheets of most formes to check for errors. (This practice varied widely from one printing house to another and from book to book within a given printing house.) We know that those in the printing trade were much more likely to detect flaws in layout (e.g., broken rules or ornaments) than to attempt to ensure the accuracy of the text. Until the middle of the seventeenth century, at the earliest, it was not common to send out any sort of author's proofs, but the author was often welcomed into the printing house to check sheets at an early stage in the printing process. If the printer's proofreader or the author detected errors, the press would be stopped and the errors corrected. But it evidently was not normal, unless the problem was of considerable size and importance, to dispose of the sheets that had already been printed. The author or proofreader could even check the sheet after the first stop-press correction had been made and discover another needed change, producing yet another layer of stop-press correction. Thus, any side of any leaf of a book from the handpress period may present not only a new state of the text produced by the compositors, transferring the words of their manuscript copy into type, but also a second version of printed text produced by stop-press correction, and then a third layer produced by another stop-press correction. A further complication is that the sheets containing all the various versions of the text would have been gathered and bound indiscriminately in copies of the book eventually offered for sale.

The practice of sending out author's proofs before printing commenced certainly changed the amount of stop-press correction found in printed books,

but even the works of twentieth-century novelists may contain such corrections. If our hypothetical author lived in the later portion of the handpress
period, he probably would have corrected several sets of proofs (Edmund
Burke once demanded nine), thus producing further versions of the text. And
the published book, incorporating the changes indicated by the author's proofs,
would yield yet another. Had the author lived in the earlier period there might
not have been any marked author's proofs, and the only evidence of proofing
would be found in the stop-press corrections, if any.

Having gotten out the first edition—in quarto, say—of our hypothetical
work, let us expand our diagram to indicate how much longer our textual
history has become (historical variations, such as author's proofs, are shown
in brackets).

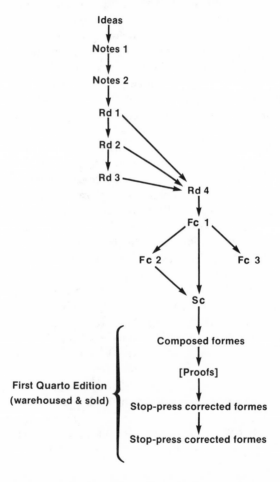

Fig. 9. Textual transmission, from ideas to first edition.

The reader should bear in mind that each point on the diagram represents a distinct and unique version of the text and should note that the first quarto edition is not, textually, a single entity at all but rather an amalgam of versions of the text.

Let us suppose that the work turns out to be unexpectedly popular, so the printer-publisher does two rather common things: has the compositors set a new edition, this time using a copy of the printed quarto as setting copy, and has a new title page set and printed with a more current date and the words "Newly revised and augmented" printed on it. This title page is inserted in all remaining unsold copies of the first quarto edition, and the original title page is removed and discarded. The publisher then markets the remaining copies of the first quarto edition as though they were a revision, even though they are the same sheets printed some months before and have been neither "newly revised" nor "augmented" in any way save for the addition of a new title page. If the printer-publisher is lucky, the shop will have reset the work (probably line for line) and printed a new supply of copies by the time the stock of old sheets has been exhausted. This is then put on the market looking, to the untrained eye, just like more copies of the "doctored" remainder sheets of the first quarto edition.

Of the textual situation that now exists at least two aspects are worth remarking on. First, because the author has had nothing to do with the text of his work since the proofreading stage, the version produced by the line-for-line reprint based on some copy of the first quarto edition will have all the readings of the first setting, the first stop-press corrections, or the second stop-press corrections (depending on which particular version of a given forme happens to be bound up in the copy used for setting the reprint), plus all those errors made by the compositors while setting the reprint. The reprint can represent only a further decay of the author's text. Second, if the first edition stocks happen to survive a little longer than was expected and are thus in the warehouse when the printed sheets from the reprint begin to arrive, then copies of the work could exist with these permutations: cancel title page with sheets of first quarto edition, cancel title page with sheets of first quarto edition and reprint mixed, reprint title page with sheets of the first quarto and reprint mixed, reprint title page with sheets of the reprint. No copies will contain the original title page, and it is unlikely that any will contain only reprint sheets headed by the cancel title page, since the reprint title page would form an integral part of the preliminary reprint sheets. Our diagram can now be expanded (see next page).

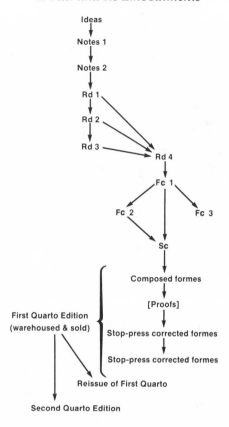

Fig. 10.   Textual transmission, from ideas to second edition.

Let us now assume that this mixed batch of sheets in the warehouse continues to sell well and that in a few years another edition is required. This time the printer-publisher asks the author if he would like to revise his work. Normally, the author would take a copy of the printed edition and mark it up with his revisions. Were he to use a copy with mixed sheets from the first and second quarto editions, the textual situation might be very confusing, though eventually rather straightforward to explain. However, let us assume that the author decides to make rather sweeping changes and produces another manuscript, without consulting any of the printed editions, states, or issues. He would, of course, consult his own notes and fair copy, but essentially he creates a new version of the work. Naturally, there would be at least one rough draft followed by at least one fair copy for the compositors. From this new, though related, start another version of the text is born in the production of the fair copy and yet another when the compositor sets the manuscript into type. Then the same processes of proofing, stop-press corrections, and the like will occur.

The popularity of the work continues, and the printer-publisher now decides to produce, without consulting the author, a cheap octavo edition. The compositors simply set line for line from a single copy of the third quarto edition (page-for-page setting would not be feasible given the change in format), and the octavo is published without proofing or checking of any kind. Again, of course, any possible combination of corrected and uncorrected sheets might be present in the copy chosen for setting this edition.

Popularity now begins to wane, and many years pass before another edition is called for. The printer-publisher either dies or retires and transfers the copyrights to another printer-publisher, and the next published edition is a duodecimo, set from a copy of the second quarto edition. Again, no proofing or authorial intervention occurs, and the final form of the diagram is as follows:

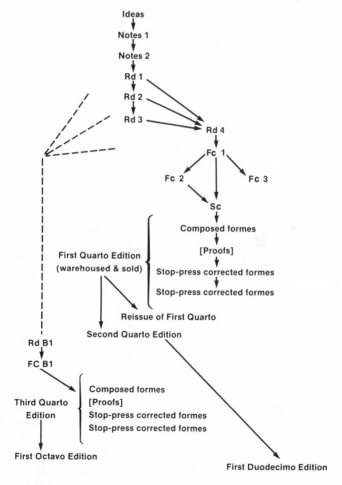

Fig. 11. Textual transmission, from ideas through five editions.

Obviously, the life of a text can be complex, but textual criticism, assisted by the methods and evidence of analytical bibliography, can recover much of it from the surviving documents and from secondary evidence. It should be apparent that the history of the text is closely linked to that of the documents that contain it, though one should not assume that the chronology of the physical documents necessarily corresponds to that of the text itself. The text in a particular document may mix early and late readings, and late documents may contain early states of the text. It is also clear that at each stage of the transmission, the text is likely to undergo alterations—in this example by the author, colleagues, scribes, printers, and compositors. Some of the alterations are corrections and revisions in the eyes of their makers; others occur more or less by happenstance, as slips of author's, scribes', and compositors' eyes, pens, minds, or fingers. The transmission does not occur in isolation from its historical circumstances, for it has been affected by the author's popular reception, by the author's relations to several audiences (patron, colleagues, and wider public), and by the methods of printing and publishing at the time.

THE LIFE OF A TEXT FROM THE MACHINE-PRESS PERIOD

At the outset this hypothetical work also exists only as ideas and notes in the author's mind and hand, but eventually it will be placed in a more formal setting. For variety we will assume that our author lives after the invention and perfection of the typewriter, so the first version of this text is the author's rough-draft typescript (Rdt). The rough draft contains the inevitable typographical errors, which the author may or may not correct at the time or subsequently, as well as second thoughts, additions, deletions, and the like made by the author in pen or pencil. At the end of this draft our author has a very rough and dirty but more or less readable typescript. She produces neither a carbon nor any sort of photocopy of the typescript. Since her typing is not great she revises a little more by hand and by typing extra sheets and then sends the work off to a professional typist who produces a clean typescript (Pt) and a carbon (Ptc).

For reasons perhaps only explained by the doctrine of original sin, the author then contrives to mix the carbon sheets with the ribbon sheets so that she has two complete copies of the professional typescript, each containing some of the carbon and some of the ribbon pages (Ptc 1 and Ptc 2). This situation is interesting because no matter how careful and professional the typist, some errors made and corrected in the ribbon copy will not be corrected in the carbon, so that Pt and Ptc will represent two different forms of the text rather than two identical copies.[25] The author has produced, by mixing carbon and ribbon copies, the same sort of situation that we observed in the mixing of sheets of the first and second quarto editions in our handpress-period example.

The author now carefully revises one of the typescripts, Ptc 1, let us say, and submits it to a publisher. The publisher agrees to publish the work, and

Ptc 1 is now subjected to the scrutiny of the publisher's editor; the result is another version of the text that carries the house styling and the wishes of the publisher and editorial staff (PubEd). Although four different versions of the text are involved (namely, ribbon copy, carbon copy, authorially revised mixed ribbon and carbon copy, and publisher-edited copy), there is only one physical object—Ptc 1. The four versions of the text exist as typewriter impressions, carbon images, author's handwriting, and editor's handwriting on the same sheets of paper.

The edited and revised typescript now is sent out for typesetting. The result, yet another version of the text because of the changes introduced by the compositor, is galley proofs (Gal). These are read by both the author and the publisher (RGal) and returned to the compositor for correction. After imposing the type into formes, the compositor produces another set of proofs— page proofs (PPro)—which are also read by the publisher and the author (RPPro) and returned for further correction.

Finally, the work is printed, bound, and put on sale. This is the first edition (1st ed) of the work and the first form in which the author's usual audience has seen it. Before printing started, however, the publisher had the printer make three sets of stereotype plates, putting two (Pl 1 and Pl 2) in storage and using the third to print this edition. Three different times the printer is asked to print copies of the work, so that the original typesetting, in plate form, is put on the press and printed at three distinct periods of time, creating three impressions of the first edition. Subsequently, the title page, dedication, and a few other parts of the printed book are altered for a variety of reasons, and the printer again mounts the plates on the press and prints a revised fourth impression of the first edition.

Later, the author takes a copy of this revised impression and marks it up extensively with changes, revisions, and corrections. The publisher uses this copy to have a second edition set and printed but does not request any proofs. Over the years plates of this setting of type are used at five different times to produce five impressions, until the plates become so worn that they will no longer print satisfactorily. At this point the publisher takes Pl 1 from storage, has the title page changed to reflect the later date and to state that this is the "Third Edition," and has copies of the book printed. But in truth this is the fifth impression of the first edition, not the third edition, and it represents a state of the text that has been supplanted by both the second edition and the revised fourth impression of the first edition.

Because damage occurs to Pl 1, the publisher brings Pl 2 out of storage and alters the title page to call this the "Fourth Edition," but it is really the sixth impression of the first edition. Several years later the work is reset from a copy of the "Fourth Edition," and this resetting is used to print an actual third edition. Even later, the new technique of photo-offset printing is used to produce more copies, which are, in effect, the second impression of the third edition.

Toward the end of her life the author so thoroughly changes her conception of her work that she writes an entirely new rough draft (NRdt) and has a typist produce a ribbon copy (NPt) and a carbon (NPtc). This time NPt goes directly from typist to publisher, is edited into compositor's copy by the publisher's staff (NPubEd), and is set into galleys (NGal). The publisher happily advertises the imminent publication of a completely revised edition. The author dies before she can read the galleys, but the publisher reads them and uses them as the basis for the fourth edition, called "Fifth Edition, newly revised" on the title page.

All this can be represented diagrammatically as follows:

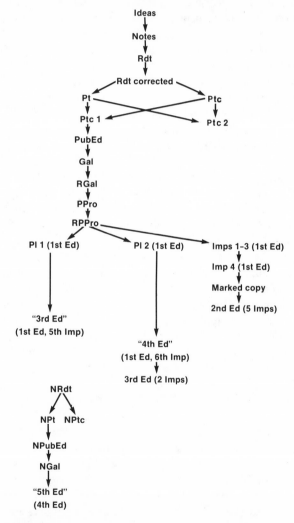

Fig. 12. Textual transmission, from ideas through four editions.

This example, like that of the handpress period, indicates the potential complexity of textual transmission. We could easily have made it more complicated by adding serialization, adaptation for film, expurgation or other alteration for another audience (or market), simultaneous or later publication in another country, and selection by book clubs. It is a prevalent but mistaken notion that textual variation, common in the handpress period, is relatively rare in the machine-press period. Although individual impressions from the machine-press period tend to be uniform, there is often wide variation between impressions and between editions. Furthermore, an author's initial (if not final) notion of a text ready for publication may differ greatly from a publisher's. In the machine-press period, plating and photographic reproduction as well as altered forms of publication may add new wrinkles, but we still see generally the same face of textual transmission.

Determining the history of textual transmission from either period requires answers to the same questions: What are the stages of transmission represented by what documents? What state of a text descended from what other or others (what served, for example, as compositor's copy)? What alterations were made before and during reproduction (whether in a printing house or a scriptorium)? What or who caused alterations? These questions are central to textual criticism and thus to scholarly editing: before a text can be established, its history must be known.

5.

Textual Criticism

Taking as its subject the transmission of texts, textual criticism lies midway between literary criticism, which focuses on works, and bibliography, which focuses on books as books. It seeks to identify the texts of a work and their various states, determine the relations between the texts, discover the sources of textual variation, and establish a text on a scholarly basis.

The term "text" is currently fashionable in literary criticism, often being used now where words like "novel," "poem," and "work" once appeared. Textual critics, however, generally use the term in a narrower sense, to refer to a work's letters, words, capitalization, punctuation, and so forth. Still, even textual critics suffer somewhat from confusion. One editor recently sought to justify an edition of Shakespeare that would present the plays in modernized or regularized spelling and punctuation. It would, he said, aid readers in exploring Shakespeare's "text." Yet spelling and punctuation are part of the text— at least in the sense that most textual critics use the term. Employing the language of semiotics, perhaps we can say that the primary interest of textual critics is not the text as sign (consisting of signifier and signified) but the text as signifier. The focus of textual criticism is on wording, not meaning. Yet it is the possibility of something's having meaning that makes it textual, that makes it a signifier. Thus lineation is considered textual in poetry, though not generally in prose. Italicization is textual unless it results merely from a printer's running short of roman type. A book set in ten-point Baskerville type could contain the same text as one set in twelve-point Caslon; thus typeface and type size are not generally thought to be textual: they are features, instead, of particular documents. (Some authors, like Laurence Sterne, have played with the conventions that separate text and documents.)

Though its eye is on the text, textual criticism cannot ignore literary criticism and analytical bibliography. As A. E. Housman said, "Because a man is not a born critic, he need not therefore act like a born fool; but when he engages in textual criticism, he often does."[26] Generally, a critical rather than a purely textual or bibliographical concern motivates textual study in the first place. Moreover, criticism defines the text by identifying the work, for texts are *of* works. Are the variant versions of Marianne Moore's "Poetry" merely variant forms of the same text, or do they really represent distinct works? The question is critical, but it has textual implications; its answer will determine whether one or several texts need to be edited. Moreover, evaluating textual variants requires critical judgment. In establishing the text of Melville's *Typee*, for instance, the editors had to determine largely on a critical basis which variants in the American revised edition resulted from the publisher's demand for expurgation and which from Melville's efforts at more nearly realizing his own conception of the work.

Another example of the application of criticism can be manufactured out of a comment in Barbara Herrnstein Smith's *Poetic Closure.* Smith says that the final words of John Donne's epigram "Hero and Leander" are "so strongly determined by all that precedes them (including, of course, the title), that one could hardly imagine how the epigram might have been otherwise concluded."[27] Now suppose that the epigram came down to us with some tatter in its mortal dress—with a lacuna that denied us the "strongly determined" words.

Both rob'd of aire, we both lye in one ground,
Both whom one fire had burnt, _____ .

If we are good critics, we should be able to repair the text by filling the blank, relying on our knowledge of the epigrammatic conventions and of the linguistic usage and metrical conventions of the period and author and on our sensitivity to poetic form and language generally. Our experience in the classroom is that some students can indeed imagine how the epigram might have otherwise concluded ("the worms go round," "the gods confound," "are toasty brown"); but many arrive at the correct answer, and many others at least recognize its superiority: "one water drownd." Though, as Bowers says, "to disbar critical judgment from the editorial process would be an act of madness," such judgment that defies or ignores bibliographical findings is madness too. Bibliography is especially useful in determining the temporal sequence of textual variation and often can reveal which readings are authoritative. In Melville's *White-Jacket*, one might on critical grounds prefer a misprint ("soiled fish" for "coiled fish"), but it remains a misprint.[28] If bibliography cannot always make the judgment, it can usually delimit the area in which judgment must be applied.

Moreover, textual criticism—or at least that part known as critical editing—is concerned with what authors intended to write, not with what, according to some aesthetic principle, they should have written. Not all textual critics have resisted the temptation to tinker and to try their hands at creation rather than emendation. In his 1732 edition of Milton's *Paradise Lost*, for example, Richard Bentley noted that in Book 4,

Ithuriel here finds a *Toad* in Adam's Bower; and so very presuming as to sit close at *Eve's* Ear, while she lay asleep! This alone might discover him to be *Satan,* before he touch'd him with his Spear. For we know, the Bower was sacred and sequestered to *Adam* and *Eve* only; IV.703.

> *Other Creature there,*
> *Beast, Bird, Insect or Worm, durst enter none.*

This the Two Angels could not be ignorant of: and therefore why may not I add *one* Verse to *Milton,* as well as his Editor add so *many:* especially, since I do not do it clandestinely. . . .

So add he does, putting a real toad of a line into Milton's imaginary garden:

> Him thus intent Ithuriel with his spear
> Knowing no real Toad durst there intrude,
> Touch'd lightly: for no falshood can endure
> Touch of Celestial temper. . . .

The second line is Bentley's.[29] It is now part of the history of Milton's text and is itself a subject for textual criticism, which in its broadest sense is not limited to establishing what an author wrote. As the study of the history of texts, it also addresses other questions: How did an author revise the text? What texts were available to readers at a particular time—for example, when an author's reputation was being established? How did editors of various periods alter texts to satisfy their aesthetic, moral, or other principles? How have economic considerations affected the texts? Textual criticism is a historical study and thus sees texts in relation to historical events and forces.

Still, the ultimate aim of textual criticism is generally thought to be the production of scholarly editions. Not all editing, of course, is scholarly. Publishing firms employ a variety of editors to "improve" texts. Thus editors at Macmillan and then at Appleton-Century collaborated with Willard Motley to reduce his 600,000-word typescript of *Knock on Any Door* to 250,000 words, to eliminate parts of the novel they judged wooden, to soften the depiction of sexuality and political corruption, and to manufacture a book that they could market at three dollars a copy. Their main concern was not fidelity to Motley's wording but creation of a marketable product. Most such editors remain in the shadows though some, like Maxwell Perkins, become as well known as the authors whose works they midwife. Some nonscholarly editions—usually reprints of standard literary works—put on an air of scholarship by having noted critics introduce or "edit" the text. Unfortunately, many textbooks—or trade books used as textbooks—fit this category. The texts they contain are often corrupt.[30]

Scholarly editing, however, is based on textual scholarship. It takes two major forms: documentary editing and critical editing. Documentary (or diplomatic) editing aims to reproduce a manuscript or printed text as a historical artifact. Such editing is noncritical in that it does not emend the text, even a text that may not accurately reproduce an author's words. The First Quarto of *Hamlet* is a "bad" quarto, probably based on a memorial reconstruction by one or more actors. Its text, though not authoritative, is of interest and can be made accessible through a diplomatic edition. So too can the texts of an author's letters, journals, and other papers; in fact, documentary editing is the method of choice for texts that their authors did not prepare or intend to prepare for publication. Scholarly editing is not limited to literary works: in recent years historians have become more aware of their need for soundly edited texts, often in documentary editions. This sort of editing aims for exact fidelity to the text's wording, spelling, punctuation, and the like. To alter them is to tamper with the text as a historical document. If F. Scott Fitzgerald spelled poorly in his letters, we want to see it. If the First Quarto of *Hamlet* reads "sallied flesh" rather than "sullied flesh" or "solid flesh," then the diplomatic text must read "sallied." One means of presenting such a text is through a facsimile, which preserves (if carefully made) much of the extratextual physical detail of the document, including typography, lineation of prose, and spacing. A "diplomatic reprint," however, preserves only the text—the wording, spelling, punctuation, and so forth.

Another alternative, a variorum edition, presents a text as it exists in several documents. Such an edition transcribes a base text from one document and, in notes or some other form of apparatus, records the textual variants from the other documents. Thus, for their three-volume textual variorum of Whitman's *Leaves of Grass* (New York: New York Univ. Press, 1980), Sculley Bradley and his fellow editors selected as a base text that of the final authorized impression of the 1881 edition, and they noted chronologically all variant readings from the previous editions. The variorum thereby allows a reader to see the complex thirty-year progress of *Leaves of Grass*—its development, additions, deletions, conflations, revisions, and groupings and regroupings of poems. Such an edition is documentary rather than critical; in other words, it does not emend the text, even a text known to contain errors (as in fact the *Leaves* base text does).

A single document, of course, can contain several states of a text. Manuscripts, for example, often contain crossings out, interlineations, multiple readings, and the like. These states can be rendered in "genetic transcription," which employs various symbols to record the textual variation and its chronology. Unpublished in Melville's lifetime, *Billy Budd* comes to us in a semifinal draft. There was no satisfactory edition until 1962, when the University of Chicago Press published both a "reading text" and a "genetic text" edited by Harrison Hayford and Merton M. Sealts, Jr. The reading text is a product of critical editing; the genetic text, of documentary editing. For the genetic text, Hayford and Sealts made a literal transcript of the manuscript, leaf by leaf. The base for the transcription is the earliest version of each of the 370 leaves. They reported the numerous revisions found on the leaves as bracketed interruptions and identified each revision according to the stage of revision it represents.

The result, then, is not a mere transcription, itself an often difficult task in documentary editing, but a transcription that reflects painstaking analysis of how Melville went about developing his story. And just as the editors of the variorum *Leaves of Grass* employed analytical bibliography to untangle a complex printing history of multiple editions and impressions and thus to identify correctly the documents that contained the evolving text, so too did Hayford and Sealts resort to physical analysis of Melville's manuscript. By identifying the several stocks of paper, matching the edges of leaves cut and torn from larger sheets, and tracing the various colors of Melville's ink, crayon, and pencil, they were better able to establish the chronology of revision.

Other formats or combinations of formats for documentary editions include photofacsimile and literal transcription on facing pages and transcription of variant states in parallel columns. Common to all, though, is the intention to report as accurately and clearly as possible the texts of documents as historical artifacts.

Critical editing, the second major form of scholarly editing, does not reproduce the text of a particular document but produces an eclectic text based on several texts and on editorial emendations. It assumes that though the multiple texts of a work may vary in authority, no one text is entirely authoritative. Until the twentieth century, this sort of editing was dominated by classical and biblical studies and was applied, at least in its sophisticated form, to classical and vernacular texts that had been transmitted over centuries through manuscripts. For Ovid's *Metamorphoses*, there are some five hundred manuscripts; for the New Testament, some five thousand. Scholars have developed various methods for such texts and to some extent have adapted them to texts transmitted through print. One of the earliest, called the eclectic method, called for assembling the various states of a text, discovering their textual variants, and then selecting those readings that met some criterion. An advance over this technique was the stemmatic or genealogical method, also called the Lachmannian method, after one of its nineteenth-century practitioners. This method has three interrelated parts: (1) *recensio*, the study of the manuscript tradition so as to construct a family tree, or stemma, and to reconstruct an "archetype" to which the other texts are "witnesses"; (2) *examinatio*, the determination of the authority of the texts and their variant readings: (3) *divinatio*, the conjectural emendation to correct errors. Evidence for the stemma derives largely from common errors between manuscripts (common errors indicating common ancestry), striking agreements or disagreements between manuscripts, directional variants (such as the "frantick" example on p. 23), and the chronology and provenance of the manuscripts. In the twentieth century, aided by computers and statistical methods, some textual critics have employed a stemmatics based more on an analysis of textual variation (a calculus of variants) than on the genealogy of particular states of texts as embodied in particular manuscripts.

But editors of postclassical texts face a somewhat different situation. Generally, the earliest document containing their text is not separated from the original by many centuries and many lost manuscripts. And the text has often been formally published and transmitted through print. Stemmatics remains important, but analytical bibliography plays a more crucial role. The editing of such texts is our chief concern here.

A critically edited text, when combined with an apparatus that presents the evidence used in the text's construction and that lists the variants of the authoritative states, is called a "critical edition." Since critical editions are eclectic, their editors must have some principle of eclecticism, some basis on which to judge the authority of the variant readings and states of the text and on which to make emendations. Several bases are possible, each depending on a different concept of textual authority. Especially in the manuscript culture, for example, it seems that the work rather than the text often held dominant authority. The spirit mattered more than the letter, and thus the text might gain accretions and alterations that would not be considered corruptions. There are also the authority of popularity, the validation of a text by the process of its consumption or by its function in a community rather than by its original creation; the authority of literary and linguistic convention, which sometimes has led editors to regularize and normalize an author's metrics or word order or whatever (often according to the conventions of the editor's time rather than the author's); and the authority of the document (the manuscript or book), which is primary in documentary editing. Tracing the history of a text often reveals how these and other sources of authority have contended with one another and left their mark.

In critical editing, however, authorial intention is the dominant authority. Of course, accepting authorial intention as a basis for editing raises difficult theoretical and practical questions and especially in recent years has provoked much debate. How, for example, is intention to be determined? Should we infer it primarily from the text itself or from an author's statements about the text? Is there more than one intended text? Do we want the hieratic text that the author intended for circulation among friends or the demotic text intended for a wider public? Do we want the theatrical text or a text freed from the influence of performance? Was an author indifferent to some textual variation or instability? At what point do an author's revisions create not a variant text but a new work? Should an author be considered an autonomous authority, or should textual authority be expanded to include the historical circumstances of literary production and publication that have influenced the text? Answers to such questions will vary, for they depend, after all, on the editor's purpose and critical judgment. Critical editing establishes not so much *the* text as *a* text of a work, generally the one that, according to editorial judgment, represents what the author intended. Since authors often engage in correction and revision (before and after initial publication), the text has been that which the author is believed to have *finally* intended, although it is also possible to edit critically a text according to what the author intended at any point in its development.

The method of critical editing, then, is (1) to discover the variant readings of a text and to adopt those that represent the author's final intention and (2) to detect erroneous (i.e., nonauthorial) readings and to correct them by proposing readings that more accurately represent what the author intended to write. To accomplish this, an editor selects a "copy-text"—the one state of the text that is determined to be most authoritative—and then emends it. Generally, the copy-text is an early state (contained in the holograph manuscript, proofs, or first printed state), for though later states may contain an author's corrections and revisions, they also are likely to contain corruptions introduced during the process of transmission. In some cases, particularly during the two centuries after the advent of printing, substantial numbers of manuscript copies were created, either by the author or by others. Many of these manuscripts were produced before or during the printing of the work, and all such manuscript transmissions may introduce variants. In these instances the textual critic may find not a regular linear descent of the text but clusters, or classes, of manuscripts that contain similar readings and that form families of texts much in the way ancient texts do. A common further complication is the publication of several printed editions, each of which may derive from a different manuscript family. Although textual critics perform the same basic operations for these texts as for those whose primary existence is linear, they must take into account a more varied and complex manuscript tradition.

When it is not known whether readings in the early state are the most authoritative, they are still presumed authoritative, according to W. W. Greg's "The Rationale of Copy-Text"—again because of the general rule that later states, though they may contain revisions, also contain corruptions.[31] Thus, in constructing a critical text, the editor retains the readings of the copy-text unless there is evidence that variant readings of later states are authorial. Textual authority, as Greg pointed out, is often divided: authorial and nonauthorial readings can exist in the same state of a text. Adopting some readings from one state does not require uncritical adoption of its others. Editors are especially likely to find a division of authority between what Greg called, somewhat misleadingly, the "accidentals" (spelling, punctuation, capitalization, etc.) and the "substantives" (wording). Generally, later states of a text are likely to be less authoritative in accidentals than in substantives, because most authors pay less attention to accidentals and because compositors and others involved in printing and publishing or in the copying of manuscripts feel more free to alter them. Thus, lacking evidence to the contrary, editors retain the accidentals of the copy-text, even if a later state of the text has the more authoritative substantive readings. If they could establish the authority of the accidentals and substantives of every state, editors would not need a copy-text: they would simply construct a text from all the authoritative readings. But seldom is there sufficient evidence to indicate the authority of every reading. Thus, faced with readings of indeterminate authority, editors rely on the copy-text to provide readings that are likely to be authoritative.

In practice, decisions about textual authority are usually difficult. Evidence is scarce for many texts. The development of analytical bibliography is in part a result of this scarcity. Often with remarkable results, it attempts to glean as much evidence as possible from the physical embodiments of texts. But even when substantial other evidence survives in the form of an author's drafts, correspondence with publishers, and the like, difficulties remain. Authors themselves may intervene in their texts in ways that are corrupting, that do not fulfill their intentions. When, at his publisher's insistence, Melville struck certain passages from *Typee* for the revised American edition, the result was an edition he himself called "expurgated"; the deletions seem not to represent his intention (though certain other changes in the edition do).[32] At the same time, publishers and compositors can serve as authors' agents and aid them in fulfilling their intentions. Discovering that a printer's proofreader was tampering with his punctuation, Mark Twain said that he "telegraphed orders to have him shot without giving him time to pray." But many authors have depended on corrections or alterations by copy editors, compositors, proofreaders, and others. Thus some "nonauthorial" readings may in fact be part of the text as an author intended it. Only by considering all available evidence and by carefully and openly dealing with whatever difficulties arise can textual scholars produce satisfactory critical editions.

Situated somewhere between these two major forms of scholarly editing—that is, between documentary and critical editing—is what Hans Zeller has called "historical-critical editing."[33] Its chief aim is to provide a complete textual history rather than to establish a text. Historical-critical editing, which recently has found favor among German textual critics, sees textual authority residing more in the states than in the individual readings of a text. To produce an eclectic text is to violate this authority and create a contaminated text. Each state of a text—that is, each combination of readings—is a version. Not all versions, of course, have equal authority, since their authority varies according to whether the author commissioned, supervised, proofread, accepted, or was otherwise involved with them. The historical-critical editor selects one "authorized" version and then uses it as a base, presenting the remaining versions in an apparatus. (If no version is authorized, the editor selects the version nearest in line of transmission to a lost authority.) Yet this is not strictly documentary editing. It allows emendation, though only for a "textual fault," which Zeller defines as "an intermittent suspension of authorisation" (p. 260). Textual faults exist only when the reading in question (1) violates sense and textual structure and (2) arises from a suspension of authorization demonstrated by analytical bibliography. (Thus not all misprints are textual faults, for some may be subsequently authorized.) Moreover, the method permits emendation only when the correction is unequivocal. This kind of editing supposedly avoids the problem of determining an author's intentions and of distinguishing between aesthetic and other intentions. Thus it is beside the point whether the expurgated version of Melville's *Typee* contains variants that fulfill his artistic conception of the work and variants that represent his reluctant acquiescence to his publisher's demand to soften or cut offensive passages. The expurgated version, like the earlier nonexpurgated version, is authorized. And, in the view of historical-critical editing, to produce an edition that combines readings from the versions is to create a version without authority.

CRITICAL EDITING

In the Anglo-American tradition of textual criticism, critical editing is most often used for texts that their authors intended for publication, whether in print or in manuscript. For this reason and because some of its methods (especially its study of textual transmission and variation) apply to other forms of textual study and scholarly editing, we will describe in some detail how critical editions are prepared.

Since the concern of the textual critic is the text in its various embodiments, as well as that form of the text most closely representing the author's final intention, the first task of the editor preparing a critical edition is to assemble a list of all the extant copies of all the significant forms of the text. Although this might at first appear straightforward, opinions vary widely on the necessity of obtaining and including certain types of material and on how to assemble the forms of the text. The financial support for textual studies in the humanities being what it is, most scholars these days find it more convenient to compile a master file of microfilm or xerographic copies of the relevant texts than to travel about the world spending as much time at a given library as it takes to collate all the texts located there. However, scholars should be aware that no matter how good a reproduction of a document may be, it is never a substitute for consulting the actual document and that editors will ultimately have to check any edition prepared from film or photocopies against the originals if they wish to avoid problems. For example, George Walton Williams and Thomas L. Berger have pointed out, with the assistance of Neil Taylor, that several misreadings in T. H. Howard-Hill's *Oxford Shakespeare Concordance* for *Henry IV, Part II* derived from blots or stains on the originals that produced apparently different words when only a photographic facsimile was employed.[34] It is also true that a fair amount of research must be devoted simply to discovering the locations of the desired copies and ascertaining that they have not been sold, moved, put on permanent loan, or lost. Although standard reference guides and bibliographies are of great assistance in such matters, the scholar may, or rather should, eventually write to likely libraries and use the free ads provided in the pages of many learned journals to request this kind of information.

Assuming that the scholar has successfully compiled a complete list of forms of the text and locations of copies of the various forms, he or she must now decide how to deal with them. The editor will certainly want to use any forms of the text that are written or corrected in the author's own hand (manuscripts, typescripts, notebooks, proofs, and the like), as well as the printed forms of the text done within the author's life or over which the author's intended revisions may have had some control (the *Miscellaneous Poems* of Andrew Marvell or all the works of Sir Philip Sidney, save the *Defence of Poesy*, are good examples of the latter instance). For texts with an extensive manuscript tradition, the editor will want to consider not only manuscript material in the author's own hand but all the manuscripts dating from the author's lifetime—and in some cases well after it—to determine whether readings in this manuscript tradition derive from original authorial manuscripts and from revisions of such manuscripts by the author. Although this kind of problem most often dates from the first two centuries after the appearance of printing, it can occur at any time, as the complex manuscript (and proof) situation surrounding the publication of James Joyce's *Ulysses* demonstrates.

Next, the question arises concerning how many copies of a given edition should be collated. For most editions produced before 1660 so few copies survive into our own times that the answer is usually simple: all the surviving copies. But for most works after 1660—and for some few before—so many copies survive that it becomes utterly impractical to collate all. Current discussion has settled on some number between twelve and twenty because the chances of discovering further press variants after collating this number diminishes to an insignificant statistical probability. One might choose to collate only ten copies of a particular edition but to check all obtainable copies at those spots where changes have been found or uncorrected errors observed, or one might select random samples in the edition and collate them against all, or nearly all, surviving copies. Or one might give over the remainder of a career and collate all the surviving copies of all the various editions of some text like Saul Bellow's *Herzog*. In any event, the textual scholar must decide at the outset, and the decision must be plausible. Next, the editor should secure the copies that must be consulted or arrange to visit all the locations of these copies, for he or she must now begin collating these texts, that is, comparing them symbol for symbol and recording any differences (see Appendix on Textual Notation).

Although the actual process of collation is uniform, it serves two distinct purposes, and thus we will speak as though there were two separate processes, one "horizontal" and the other "vertical." In the first, the horizontal comparison of texts, the editor collates with one another the copies produced from each individual setting (whether directly from type or indirectly through plates)— in other words, all those copies that are part of a single edition, as defined by analytical bibliography, whether or not they also form part of the subsets called impressions, issues, or states. The reason for undertaking this work is (1) to determine whether an edition contains stop-press corrections and if so to determine which of the readings produced by each correction is the "corrected" reading[35] or (2) to determine whether textual alterations were made between the various impressions of an edition and if possible to ascertain the source of the corrections. Since throughout the handpress period it was the normal practice not to dispose of the already printed sheets that contained uncorrected readings, surviving copies of the book are as likely to carry uncorrected readings as they are to carry corrected ones. Even in the modern era printers and publishers occasionally produce works that contain sheets with uncorrected readings, and since the advent of plating later impressions are often printed from plates that have been corrected to some degree. Thus, whether the alterations were done on the bed of the press during the actual printing process or done on plates or standing type between impressions, the importance of the evidence and the purpose and means for discovering it remain the same.

Collating procedures for a text transmitted through manuscript resemble those for multiple copies of a single printed edition. That is, the editor tries to determine which variants exist only because of the process of copying the manuscript and which are the result of the particular exemplar used to produce the manuscript. Such determinations allow the editor to group the various manuscripts into families, and the result is often similar to that for a printed book that has undergone several significant stop-press corrections.

Collation has always been a singularly dull and exacting practice. In the past few decades, however, several devices have been perfected that greatly assist, in both ease and accuracy, the process of collating multiple copies of books from one setting of type—that is, the process of horizontal comparison. The computer offers the hope of creating even better collations in the decades to come. After that optimistic introduction to the subject, we must hasten to add that most editors still follow the time-honored process of looking at two texts with the naked eye, symbol for symbol, to discover how they differ. Save for the possible application of computer technology to the process, this ancient method of collation is the only one available for vertical comparison, which is the comparison of copies from different settings of type. This nonmechanical method is prone to error, and the editor who employs it will usually want to repeat the process with any two texts several times to compensate for the collator's mental or visual errors. Certain minor sophistications are possible with this process: one might have a partner read the base text aloud while the other follows along in the second text (with world enough and money one might even have a large crew of such "followers" and one lector), or one might tape-record a spoken version of the base text and after correcting that tape use it as the lector while following along in subsequent copies of that text (this system at least reduces the potential for error caused by misspeaking). Beyond these refinements however, one must simply slog on with collations.

Editors can collate copies of a single setting of type (issues and states of an edition, impressions from the same standing type or plates, and photographic reprints) using either the Hinman collator or the Lindstrand comparator, or devices deriving from them.[36] Machine collation poses a certain logistical problem: editors must find copies of the work they intend to collate in places that possess collators or comparators, or they must obtain undistorted photocopies.[37] The Hinman collator superimposes reflected images of two copies and illuminates them with alternating light sources that cause variants—of even the smallest sort, such as broken letters—to appear to wave or blink. The Lindstrand comparator also uses reflected images but, through a central prismatic eyepiece, combines them in the user's nervous system, much as the old stereopticon did, so that variants appear to float off the page or are indecipherable blurs. Though both devices have defects as well as advantages, editors should employ them if at all possible.

In theory, the computer should bring an end to the drudgery of collating texts, but current technology still requires manual inputting for almost all texts, thus creating yet one more point of possible error in the textual process. Until optical scanners become more adept at reading an actual copy of the text and the cost of computing goes down or the funding of textual computing goes up, editors will use the computer only when their access to and interest in computers are great or when the complexity of their textual problem demands it.

Variants found in collation fall into three kinds: (1) variants created by mishaps in typesetting and printing, (2) variants created by the proofreader without reference to copy, and (3) variants created either by the author in proofreading or revising or by the proofreader with reference to the author's copy. The first sort will obviously be of no final textual consequence, but many variants created inadvertently may not appear, at first inspection, to be inadvertent. In texts printed before about 1800 damage to the cross bar of the letter *f* will produce the perfectly acceptable letter long *s*, turning such words as "funny," "fake," and "foil" into "sunny," "sake," and "soil." In books set with individual pieces of type, including modern books set by monotype, the loss of the letter *g* during either imposition or printing would produce a variant reading for the phrase "the Grecian grape." In modern books produced by compositional processes that deal with whole lines as physical units (linotype and certain kinds of photographic composition), lines can be reversed in ways that alter meaning without creating pure nonsense, as careful readers of newspaper picture captions can testify from their own experience.

Of course, a knowledge of analytical and historical bibliography is necessary to untangle some variants of this first kind, though the great majority are transparently evident. However, two points about them must be stressed. First, such inadvertent variants will appear as "corrected" readings during collation since they are chronologically subsequent to the original, or "uncorrected," readings. Second, although they have no textual authority, they often induce the printer to attempt repairs during the printing process and thus may cause the second or third kind of variant to occur. Even more extreme forms of inadvertent variants may be found in cases where an accident in the printshop destroys a few plates or a page or more of set and printed type and the printer attempts to replace the lost material by replating or by resetting page for page or line for line. Such accidents will produce either anomalous readings in the variant record or deceptive "uncorrected" and "corrected" readings, and care must be exercised using the tools of analytical and historical bibliography to ensure an accurate understanding of the entire printing process.

The second kind of variant is much like the first except that it does involve human intervention with the conscious intention to correct the text, while the first kind is purely inadvertent. However, so long as the proofreaders do not refer to the setting copy, their corrections are no more authoritative than those produced by mishap and are much less authoritative than the modern critical editor's emendations, which are based on his or her study of all the bibliographical facts and on critical judgment. Corrections made without reference to copy normally attempt to tidy up the printing, that is, to eliminate such things as turned letters, broken rules, faulty pagination or direction lines, and gross spelling errors. Experience has taught us that although such attempts may proceed deep enough into the text to correct such an error as "John" for "George," they usually do not go so deep as to correct "can not" for "can." Furthermore, since this type of correction is a true stop-press correction and involves unlocking the chase or making other alterations in the imposed forms or stored plates, any accidents in making the correction will introduce variants of the first kind. But, as with the first kind, the very existence of such variants may generate the third kind, either at the same time or later.

The third kind of variant is, of course, what the textual critic is most interested in. In this case the author, or a proofreader following the author's copy, has corrected a false reading in the text or replaced one authorial reading with another. However, as with the second kind of variant, correcting or revising the standing type or plates may introduce further unintended variants.

Separating these three kinds of variants from one another once the collation of the copies of a given edition is complete can be very complex. The editor must be constantly aware that the basic unit of press correction is the forme, that is, the type used to print one side of a sheet. Thus, if the outer forme of a gathering that shows only one instance of stop-press correction contains variants clearly of type three (a change that can only have been made by the author or by reference to the author's copy) along with variants that could be either of that type or of type two, the editor is reasonably safe in assuming that these latter variants were made at the same time and by the same agent as the former ones and thus have the same authority. Problems will certainly occur in dealing with variants produced by stop-press correction, and they require the application of critical judgment based on all the available evidence. In any event, the editor's aim is to construct an "ideal" text for each setting of the work. This ideal text, although it may be unlike any previous individual version, will embody all the most authoritative readings found in all copies of that setting.

After producing an ideal text for each edition of the work done in the author's lifetime or over which the author may have exercised any authority, the editor must collate these ideal versions and any manuscripts, corrected proofs, and the like. This set of collations, which we call the vertical comparison of texts, will reveal to the editor how the author or others may have altered the text from edition to edition, how the mere process of reproduction has introduced corruption, and how various earlier forms of the text, or completely new ones, were used as setting copy at a later time. For example, this sort of collation will reveal that after a 1647 separate quarto edition of Jeremy Taylor's *The Liberty of Prophesying*, a second and a third issue of this quarto in a collected edition of various works (1648 and 1650), a second edition in a folio collection in 1657, and a third edition in another folio collection in 1674, finally a 1702 quarto edition set from a copy of the 1647 edition appeared with the designation "The Second Edition, Corrected" on its title page. However, major changes and additions made by Taylor in 1657 and repeated in 1674 are, of course, not in the 1702 edition, which is actually the fourth edition; and since the copy of 1647 used for setting copy was randomly selected and not compared with later editions, even some of the uncorrected readings of formes in 1647 were reproduced.[38]

Now that all collations are complete the editor possesses a set of notes recording all variations, from whatever sources, along both the horizontal and the vertical axes of the text's history.

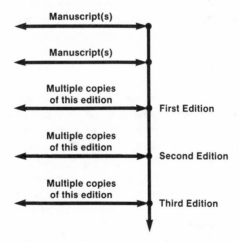

Fig. 13. Horizontal and vertical collation.

Several other steps precede the actual editing of the text. First, the editor must determine on physical grounds, or at least documentable grounds, which variants on either axis are authoritative, probably authoritative, nonauthoritative, or indifferent. Usually such sorting will also in part answer the second question: Which variants on the vertical axis are authoritative and, therefore, reflect the author's final intention? Of course, this process of determination cannot be merely mechanical, but all except the most complex or confused variants will dispose themselves into clearly defined and understandable categories. Third, the editor will want to establish a stemma, a family tree, of the work. For most texts, where external dating is clear and unambiguous, this will be fairly easy, but the history of the study of the Shakespeare quartos before Pollard and Greg's work should warn all editors to be on their guard against false datings, forgeries, and other "machinations" of publishers out for gain above all else. The stemma should account for every major form of the text (manuscripts, proofs, editions, and corrected states and impressions, though normally not variations within these forms such as stop-press corrections). The principal purpose of the stemma is to allow the reader to see at a glance and in diagrammatic form the editor's view of the genesis of the text.

In order to construct the stemma the editor will have to make some crucial determinations based on an analysis of the variants found and recorded. For example, it will be important to decide, for each form of the text, what document or documents served as compositor's or scribe's copy. Although this copy will sometimes be easy to identify, as in the case of the 1702 *Liberty of Prophesying* mentioned above, it can be quite elusive, as in the cases of Shakespeare's *Othello*, *King Lear*, or *Henry IV, Part II*. As one moves forward in history, more and more of the documents used for setting have been preserved, making the editor's job clearer, if not easier; but even in so modern a work as D. H. Lawrence's *Women in Love*, two typescripts made up of mixed ribbon and carbon copies, some corrected by Lawrence himself and some by his wife, will certainly cause some editorial concern and deliberation.

For works from earlier periods the editor will attempt to determine compositorial practices and what portions of each edition were set by what compositors. This not only provides evidence about the order in which the edition was set and printed but also sheds light on how the compositors may have altered the accidentals of the author's text. Extensive research has been carried out on the compositors of the Shakespeare quartos and First Folio and of certain other sixteenth- and seventeenth-century works, and the study of this aspect of book production is now taking in ever broader areas of the English book trade. Modern compositors have not been allowed the freedom of their colleagues of the earlier period, but the editor of modern works must still consider house style and copyediting.

The editor will also wish to investigate the proofreading of the printed editions. For early books evidence normally derives from an analysis of the stop-press corrections discovered during collation, and the work done with them has been discussed above.[39] From the later seventeenth century the practice of providing authors with proofs before printing started became ever more common, and by the eighteenth century the editor may assume that this was normal practice for any serious work, though whether the author attended to them carefully is entirely another matter. Modern publishers frequently preserve an author's correspondence and several sets of marked proofs, and in such cases the editor will of course take care to evaluate such authorial changes as likely readings for the edited text. No matter what the circumstances, the editor must bend every effort to take full account of all the changes, errors, or failures to correct associated with setting, imposing, proofing, and printing. From these and other studies of the variants of the text, the editor will eventually be able to construct a life history of the work and to establish the relationships among the individual members of that family.

The editor next confronts what can be the most vexed question in critical editing and one that can save or damn the entire effort: selection of the copy-text for the edition. The editor will normally choose that text which lies closest to the author's final intention in accidentals. Thus, if no manuscripts or corrected proofs in the author's hand survive and if all printed editions are in ancestral relationship with one another, then the editor will choose the earliest printed edition as the copy-text because it is more likely than any subsequent edition to preserve the accidentals of the text. If the author made substantive changes in subsequent editions, the editor will emend the copy-text accordingly, but such changes of words will have almost no effect on the accidentals of the text and will certainly not cause the editor to choose a different copy-text.

However, other considerations may enter in. For example, if the author in question can be demonstrated to have paid considerable attention to the accidentals—as well as, or even instead of, the substantives—of the text in every edition down to the last printed in his or her lifetime, then the editor will choose the latest edition as the copy-text, for this embodies the author's final intention in both substantives and accidentals. Or, if the author produced an entirely new manuscript or typescript from which a later edition was printed, then that later edition could contain the author's final intention and might be selected as copy-text. Another situation, common in the early drama but possible with any text, arises when the earliest edition is set from a document not produced by the author (in the drama, from a theater prompt book or a memorial transcription by a member of the theatrical company or by a scribe sent to the playhouse to take down the words of the play) and a later edition is then set from the author's manuscript. In such a case the later edition is obviously the choice for copy-text, but things are often not this straightforward.

A copy of the unauthoritative earlier edition, for example, will often be conflated with the author's manuscript, and the marked-up printed edition will serve as setting copy for the later edition. In such an instance neither the early nor the later edition will embody the author's intentions regarding the accidentals, except possibly in those passages of some length that are written into the printed copy from the author's manuscript. If the author exercises any control over the production of the later edition, selection of copy-text becomes rather arbitrary, but the editor would probably choose the later edition since it may contain authorial accidentals while the earlier edition would contain none. In any of these situations, however, the substantives would be adopted into the copy-text according to their authoritativeness no matter how the editions were produced.

In certain extreme circumstances the editor may not be able to select a single copy-text at all. The two texts of Marlowe's *Doctor Faustus* or the early-edition and New York–edition texts of Henry James's novels represent different versions of these works—or perhaps different works altogether—and thus would be edited separately, each with its own copy-text.

Having selected the copy-text, the editor must now edit the work. Except in diplomatic editions, reprintings, and documentary editing, this process is almost entirely concerned with emending the copy-text with other more authoritative readings from other documents, correcting unambiguous defects in the copy-text, and choosing from among indifferent readings or emending on the editor's own authority. We will discuss each of these three processes in turn, although it is important to note that they normally go on at the same time and that one sort of textual choice may immediately throw light on another choice in a different category.

The editor emends the copy-text with more authoritative readings from other printed and manuscript documents when the vertical collation of texts and the analysis of the recorded variants indicate that the author intervened in the transmission of the text. Practice has shown us that this most often concerns substantive readings rather than accidentals, but editors must always be alert for either sort of authorial intervention. Thus, when the results of collation clearly show that the author has introduced certain changes in the text, the editor must adopt these readings and emend the copy-text. For example, Samuel Daniel became convinced that proper poetic style demanded lines with masculine rather than feminine endings (i.e., lines ending with stressed rather than unstressed syllables). He revised his sonnet sequence *Delia* according to this conviction and also tinkered with other features of the work, eventually revising it four times. The editor faced with such a problem will adopt the substantive changes that Daniel made in the four revisions but will retain the accidentals of the earliest text containing a given sonnet.[40] For, as we said earlier, the editor seeks to produce a text that embodies, at every point, the author's final intention, and the masculine endings and other substantive revisions were certainly Daniel's final intention.

Although it is obvious that the editor will choose to incorporate an author's substantive changes into the copy-text, other textual concerns are not so clear-cut. Historical bibliography will provide the editor with much information about the operation of the publishing and printing industry during the period in question, and analytical bibliography will supply a model and a method for determining precisely how each printed version of the text was affected by the master printers, compositors, copy editors, censors, and others concerned with the production of books. Thus the editor may be in a position to emend the copy-text at various disputed points because of the detection of compositorial spelling habits, house styles, or the exigencies of having to fit a fixed amount of copy into a fixed amount of space in the printed book.[41] Shakespearean textual studies have devoted so much time to identifying compositors over the last decades that editors can isolate those accidentals and, in some cases, substantives in a text caused not by the intervention of authority but by compositorial preference or necessity. Or, for nineteenth- and twentieth-century American authors published first in Britain, the editor will wish to determine whether the American or the British spelling of such words as "colour" or "centre" has authority.

Naturally, the nature and source of the copy from which the book is set (or the manuscript is copied) is of great importance to the editor. Was the first edition set from the author's manuscript? Did the author read proofs? Was the copy a transcript at some number of removes from the author's manuscript, or was it an annotated copy of an earlier printed edition? The editor must also have a clear understanding of how the printer disposed of that setting copy. Was the copy cast off? If so, it will produce different composing, imposing, and formatting problems for the printers than will a book set serially. In books composed in the latter way, compositors will run short of space only at the ends of gatherings or the end of the book, and unauthorized changes in the text to fit the copy into the space available will occur only at these points. However, books cast off and set by formes, as was done in early printing to cut down on the amount of standing type, will have such changes at places other than the end, depending on the format of the book. Evidence supplied by analytical bibliography about the order of imposition and printing of the formes will allow the editor to avoid retaining unauthorized readings in the copy-text or, if no better reading is possible, to explain the likelihood of such readings being authorial.

Finally, however, physical evidence and bibliographical inference will sometimes fail to supply an answer. Two or more variant readings will appear to be equally possible; there will be no evidence of authorial intervention; the physical process of book production cannot logically be used to reject either reading; and no reasonable defect in the setting copy, or its source, can explain away either reading. At such points especially, textual criticism becomes *critical.* Bringing to bear a knowledge of the author, the author's style, and the style of this particular work and others like it, the editor chooses one of the variant readings on his or her own authority and defends the choice in the apparatus to the edition. Most critical editions attempt to make such decisions: they do not resort merely to the copy-text reading or to some system of parallel readings supplied perhaps in brackets.

Editors do not desire a return to that style of editing which based almost all of its textual decisions on the principle of "this is what *I* like" or "author X could not write an unmetrical line or an ungrammatical sentence, and so we will reject all unmetrical lines and ungrammatical sentences." Nor do they any longer believe that the best choice of copy-text is that of the latest edition published in the author's lifetime, unless they can prove that the author sufficiently intervened in the textual transmission to make that edition the most authoritative. Most textual choices can and must be based in large part on physical and/or external evidence, but because these bodies of evidence exist (usually in great abundance) and because literary criticism, properly practiced, provides a parallel and supportive body of evidence, the editor is not making choices blindly or by chance.

Having now chosen a copy-text and emended it according to the evidence and best judgment, the editor must decide how to present the text and its apparatus. For texts from the period of early modern English and before (approximately 1750 and back), a basic question must be answered. Will the critical text be old-spelling, regularized, or modernized? (Actually, the editor should make this decision at the beginning of the editing process, but it is more convenient to discuss it at this point.) This subject has produced a great amount of heat, and some light, in the twentieth century. Previously it was not given much consideration. For any edition, except some few intended for an exclusively antiquarian audience, most editors assumed that they should modernize everything—spelling, punctuation, paragraphing, and grammar. The rise of serious academic study of the vernacular literatures in the late nineteenth century reinforced bibliographical studies by demonstrating how much editorial practice, instead of advancing literary studies, actually impeded them. For example, many seventeenth-century prose writers had been subjected to full modernization by nineteenth-century editors, and the alteration of the punctuation had stripped their texts of the "signposts" of their rhetoric.[42] As one might expect, the reaction swung as far in the opposite direction as the practices being reacted against, and for a while diplomatic editing, verging on facsimile reprinting, was the common method used. As scholarship has regained its equilibrium, however, it has produced a scale of textual presentation that ranges from the most severe diplomatic editing through a graduated series of steps to the most freewheeling modernized editing, which is closer to adaptation than to editing.

The major forms of presentation are old-spelling, regularized, and modernized. Old-spelling editors normally present their text as faithfully as is technically possible, preserving all spelling, capitalization, italics, and the like found in the copy-text and in the texts used to emend it. This method is but one step removed from true diplomatic editing, since it allows only for emendation of the "diploma" selected as copy-text. The first step on the graduated series is usually the reduction of *f* to *s,* almost always dictated by the practical consideration that the former letter is unavailable in most modern compositors' type fonts. At the next step *i, j, u, v,* and *w* are converted to modern usage.

(In the older usage, *i* and *j* were the "same" letter, with *i* generally being used for both *i* and *j* and with *j* being used finally in combinations such as *ij*. Similarly, the use of *v* and *u* depended on position within a word and not on pronunciation, with *v* used initially, as in *vnder* [*under*] and *u* used medially, as in *euent* [*event*]. And *w* was often rendered as *uu* and *vv*.) Since these letters all exist in modern type fonts one always has the sinking feeling that this conversion results from the inability of typists, compositors, and the proofreading editors themselves to follow the older usage accurately. At this point the true old-spelling editor normally stops and will make no other silent changes in the text, although the editors of dramatic texts allow themselves further silent emendations in the dramatic paraphernalia of the text, such as speech headings and stage directions.

On the next step of the scale are the regularizing editors. They will certainly adopt all the silent changes made by the most liberal old-spelling editors and will, at least, make some silent adjustments in punctuation, capitalization, and spelling that, although not fully modernizing the text, will give it a greater internal consistency and bring it closer to modern usage. Thus regularizing editors may leave in the text old forms of words if they believe these forms might have a significance that their regularized forms would not. Obviously, this sort of editing calls for many critical judgments, none of them bibliographical. Regularized editions may be more completely altered, to the point of being what one might call "semimodernized" or "conservative modernized" editions. Such editorial work is even more critically demanding but can be very effective, as is the case with G. Blakemore Evans' *The Riverside Shakespeare*.

The final level is a fully modernized text. In these texts editors silently modernize almost everything—spelling, punctuation, and capitalization— changing to modern form just about all the accidentals of the text. Badly done, such modernization requires almost no critical judgment and might be performed by a competent copy editor in the publishing firm bringing out the edition; but well done, it requires critical sensitivity that may cause the editors to preserve important elements in the text that full modernization might obscure.

The mode of presentation may depend on the intended audience for the edition. Scholarly editions for scholarly audiences will, of course, always be in old spelling. One assumes that regularized and modernized editions are intended for the classroom or for that largely mythical figure, the general reader. However, little evidence has ever been brought forward to prove that the general reader will be more inclined to read Sir Thomas Wyatt or Michael Drayton or Fulke Greville if he is given a modernized edition. The general reader's inclination to read these authors will bring with it a willingness, if not a desire, to read them as they wrote. A special plea is often made for modernization of such major authors as Shakespeare, Donne, and Dryden, but here again the general reader is probably up to the task of reading unmodernized texts. In the classroom we seldom have students read Chaucer in modernized adaptations but insist on having him read in Middle English; and the question must arise, if Chaucer, in his original spelling, has not disappeared from the curriculum, is it likely that authors from the early modern period will vanish if they are offered in their own spelling? However, the world is wide and authors are resilient. There is room no doubt for editions of all sorts, as long as the economic dictum "bad money drives out good" does not cause modernized editions to close the market for scholarly old-spelling ones. In any case, no matter what form of textual presentation the editor chooses, the textual work lying behind the edition must be rigorous and thorough. A text must be established before it can be modernized.

Another major consideration is whether to present the edition in annotated or in clear-text form. Here the question is practical as well as academic. Sound critical editions presented in clear text—that is, with the text pages containing no annotation of any kind—are easily and practically reproducible by publishers in cheaper editions for the general reader and the classroom, and the annotations can be confined to the back of the scholarly edition. Such an arrangement allows the scholarly edition to present all the evidence and also provides for accurate cheaper editions, since in clear-text formats the publisher need not reset the text pages, thus avoiding the risk of introducing transmissional errors. However, the editor and publisher must carefully assess the potential for such cheaper publication, for many scholars have objected, and perhaps justly, to clear-text editions because the user must flip back and forth from the text to the textual notes at the end of the book.

The opposite method is to place all textual notes at the foot of the page to which they refer. With modern photo-offset printing, such an edition might still be reproducible in cheaper editions so long as no note numbers appeared in the text itself, but this method would be difficult and expensive. A middle ground adopted by some publishers is to place notes of emendation at the foot of the page and the rest of the apparatus at the end of the book. All such considerations must take into account of course the possible readership for the text.

No matter what form of presentation is adopted, any true scholarly edition must include somewhere a full textual apparatus. Although printing costs and audience will enter into these decisions, a text that does not provide an apparatus, no matter how carefully edited, is not a critical edition. Some methods of getting around costs will be suggested later.

Of course, any edition will have an introduction that places the work and author in their historical setting and that fully describes the forms of the text and the method of editing employed. All editorial conventions and silent emendations should be explained here. Normally, the introductions of scholarly editions do not engage in evaluative, interpretive, or polemical criticism.

Ideally, an apparatus should allow a user to reconstruct any form of the text, and thus it should record the history of the variants. Such a record requires the presentation of two types of evidence. The first is the historical collation, a complete record of the vertical variants of all collated forms of the text, including the present edition's emendations of the copy-text. The second is a record of the stop-press corrections, the horizontal variants, in the copy-text and in any other forms that the editor deems it necessary to present. These two items allow a user of the edition to fulfill the aim of reconstructing any form of the text. In practice, however, economic considerations often cause some compromise of the ideal. Thus many critical apparatuses record the accidentals and substantives of the copy-text but only the substantives of other authoritative texts.

The apparatus also contains a list of all emendations and a separate list of the emendations made to the accidentals of the copy-text. The reason for the first list should be obvious, but the reason for repeating the accidentals that have already been recorded in the first listing may require some explanation. Since the editors have selected their copy-text on the grounds that it represents more closely than any other texts the author's intentions regarding accidentals, they should as clearly as possible show their readers where they depart from these readings of the copy-text.

Editors of prose texts generally also include in their apparatus a list of ambiguous line-end hyphenations. The lineation of one typesetting of the text may not match the lineation of another. Thus, for example, the word "windowpane" may have been hyphenated (as "window-pane") between two lines in the copy-text but may occur unhyphenated within a line of the edited text, or vice versa. The record of such end-of-line hyphenations allows reconstruction of the copy-text and indicates whether in quoting the edited text a person should retain its particular hyphenations.

Almost any edition will contain at least one other class of information that the editor will think it important to include—a table of a particular pattern of wrong-font settings demonstrating the work of a particular compositor, reproductions of ornaments that identify an unnamed printer, or similar information. How much additional information should be included depends on how much information scholars need to use the edition properly and on the limits the publisher sets for additions to the apparatus. One way around the latter constraints is to announce in the edition that supplemental apparatus material has been deposited, in either typescript or microfilm form, in major research libraries and that copies are available at cost.

Finally, the apparatus includes discursive textual notes in which the editors argue for or explain emendations or failures to emend unexplained by the textual introduction. Depending usually on the publisher's house style and the supposed audience for an edition, the editors may also supply explanatory notes to gloss words, trace allusions and sources, and supply historical references.

Since textual apparatuses are packaged in several ways, we believe that some brief examples may be of use. The first is from Volume III of *The Dramatic*

Works of Thomas Dekker, edited by Fredson Bowers (Cambridge: Cambridge Univ. Press, 1958); the second from Volumes I and IV of *The Plays and Poems of Philip Massinger*, edited by Philip Edwards and Colin Gibson (Oxford: Clarendon, 1976); the third is from the CEAA edition of Herman Melville's works: *Mardi*, edited by Harrison Hayford, Hershel Parker, and G. Thomas Tanselle (Evanston: Northwestern Univ. Press; Chicago: Newberry Library, 1970).

THE
DRAMATIC WORKS OF
THOMAS DEKKER

EDITED BY
FREDSON BOWERS
Professor of English Literature
University of Virginia

VOLUME III

THE ROARING GIRL
IF THIS BE NOT A GOOD PLAY, THE DEVIL IS IN IT
TROIA-NOVA TRIUMPHANS
MATCH ME IN LONDON
THE VIRGIN MARTYR
THE WITCH OF EDMONTON
THE WONDER OF A KINGDOM

CAMBRIDGE
AT THE UNIVERSITY PRESS
1958

Fig. 14a. Title page: Volume III of Bowers' edition of Dekker.

Dauy.   Good tales do well,
In these bad dayes, where vice does so excell.
Adam.   Begin sir *Alexander.*
Alex.   Last day I met
An aged man vpon whose head was scor'd,
A debt of iust so many yeares as these,
Which I owe to my graue, the man you all know.
Omn.   His name I pray you sir.
Alex.   Nay you shall pardon me,   70
But when he saw me (with a sigh that brake,
Or seem'd to breake his heart-strings) thus he spake:
Oh my good knight, saies he, (and then his eies
Were richer euen by that which made them poore,
They had spent so many teares they had no more.)
Oh sir (saies he) you know it, for you ha seene
Blessings to raine vpon mine house and me:
Fortune (who slaues men) was my slaue: her wheele
Hath spun me golden threads, for I thanke heauen,
I nere had but one cause to curse my starres,   80
I ask't him then, what that one cause might be.
Omn.   So Sir.
Alex.   He paus'd, and as we often see,
A sea so much becalm'd, there can be found
No wrinckle on his brow, his waues being drownd
In their owne rage: but when th'imperious winds
Vse strange inuisible tyranny to shake
Both heauens and earths foundation: at their noyse
The seas swelling with wrath to part that fray,
Rise vp, and are more wild, more mad then they.
Euen so this good old man was by my question,   90
Stir'd vp to roughnesse, you might see his gall
Flow euen in's eies: then grew he fantasticall.
Dauy.   Fantasticall, ha, ha.
Alex.   Yes, and talkt odly.
Adam.   Pray sir proceed, how did this old man end?
Alex.   Mary sir thus.

85 winds⌄] Scott; wind, Q   93 talkt] Dyce; talke Q

Fig. 14b.   Sample page of text from Bowers' Dekker.

TEXTUAL NOTES

I.i

24 here presently, it shall]   All editors have placed a stop like a semi-colon after *here*, thus beginning a new clause with *presently*. The sense is indifferent whatever the modification, but if repetition of a cant phrase for comic effect is considered, then line 48 suggests the punctuation adopted here.

77 brow,]   Dyce and Bullen, of course, modernize to *brows* in consideration of the pronoun *them* in the next line. Nothing would be easier than for a compositor to fail to see a terminal *s*; on the other hand, Elizabethan grammar does not forbid reference of this sort.

II.ii

10 two leaud]   Collier confidently altered to *lewd*; Dyce printed *leav'd* but queried *loud;* Bullen retained *leav'd* and remarked only that the sense was intelligible. I take it that the primary sense intended is the comparison of the tongue to the two hinged parts of a door or gate, each of which can move independently and thus pronounce either slander or truth. The common phrase is 'double-tongued', or 'two-tongued', or 'fork-tongued'. The lines in Crashaw's *Hymn of the Nativity* doubtless do not apply here: 'Shee spreads the red leaves of thy Lips, | That in their Buds yet blushing lye' (*Poems*, ed. L. C. Martin [1927], p. 108).

III.iii

200 Honest Sir]   Q *Serieant* (*Seriant* [u]) is manifestly wrong. Dyce, followed by Bullen, emends to *Servant*. This is not much better, since there is small point in sounding the alarm to Gull before Jack Dapper. The odds are that the compositor mistook an abbreviation like S^r and expanded it wrongly.

IV.ii

49 Then they hang the head.]   Q prefixes the speech-heading *Mist. Open.*, which duplicates the same prefix at line 45. Line 49 begins a new page (sig. I1ᵛ). There is about a third of a line of white space after the end of the last line on sig. I1ʳ, '...animalls they are', and the catchword is '*Mist. Open.*', repeated at the first line of the next page, as '*Mist. Open.* Then they hang the head.' This line does not join very smoothly to 'Lord what simple animalls they are.' and it would seem that some brief intervening remark by Mistress Gallipot has been dropped in error, but whether by the compositor or in the manuscript is not to be determined. However, if we may trust the evidence of the catchword, the manuscript could have been at fault.

102

Fig. 14c. Sample page of textual notes from Bowers' Dekker.

PRESS-VARIANTS IN Q (1611)

[Copies collated: BM¹ (British Museum 162.d.35), BM² (Ashley 1159); Bodl (Bodleian Mal. 246[1]); Dyce (Victoria and Albert Museum); NLS (National Library of Scotland); CSmH (Henry E. Huntington Library); DFo (Folger Shakespeare Library); MB (Boston Public Library); Pforz (Carl H. Pforzheimer Collection); Taylor (Robert H. Taylor).]

SHEET A (*outer forme*)

Corrected: BM², Bodl, Dyce, NLS, CSmH, DFo, Pforz, Taylor.
Uncorrected: BM¹, MB.

Sig. A 3.
  Dedication.
  15 cod-peece] cod-peice
  15 book] booke
Sig. A 4ᵛ.
  Persons.
  Dramatis] Drammatis

SHEET B (*inner forme*)

Corrected: BM¹⁻², Bodl, Dyce, NLS, CSmH, MB, Pforz, Taylor.
Uncorrected: DFo.

Sig. B 1ᵛ.
  I.i.22 in truth ſir] intruthſir
    33 ſlakes] ſlackes
    34 faiſt] faith
    35 *viua*] *viue*
    37 What] Wthat
    39 *Neatfoote*] *Neatfootte*
Sig. B 2.
  I.i.54 Ha !] Ha:
    56 ſhape?] ſhape:
    59 prey] pray
    59 eyes] eyes,
    61 a loathed] aloathed
    78 gold] gold,
    82 heire?] heire,

104

Fig. 14d.   Sample page of press variants from Bowers' Dekker.

EMENDATIONS OF ACCIDENTALS

Dedication

hd. *Comicke*ʌ] ~ ,
15 cod-peice] Q(u); cod-peece Q(c)

15 booke] Q(u); book Q(c)
18 ha's] *text*; has *cw*

Prologue

7 *Scœne*,] ~ .

Persons

DRAMMATIS] Q(u); DRAMATIS Q(c)

I.i

16 curle-pated] curle-|pated
33–34 The more...me!] *one line in*
    Q
50 When] | when
54 Ha:] Q(u); ~ ! Q(c)
54–55 Ha! | Life...] *one line* [life] *in*
    Q
56 shape:] Q(u); ~ ? Q(c)

58–59 waite ʌ ... both,] ~ , ...
    ~ ʌ
70 broke?] ~ ,
78 me:] ~ ,
89 ship-wracke?] ~ .
106 dangerous.] dangerours,
108 about?] ~ ,

I.ii

S.D. Goshawke] Goshake
4 (At] | (at
16 Y'are] Y are
20 seemes] seeemes
21 fill'd] fiil'd
29 rarely.] ~ ,
59 A stoole.] *run-on with line* 58
87 foundation: ... noyseʌ] ~ ʌ
    ... ~ :
88 fray,] Q(u); ~ ʌ Q(c)
89 madʌ] Q(u); ~ , Q(c)
90 question,] Q(u); ~ ʌ Q(c)
94 Pray...end?] Q *lines*: proceed, |
    How

109 roote —] ~ ,
109 sonne?] ~ ,
115 subtilty —] ~ .
119 foundation —] ~ ,
124 teeth —] ~ ,
143 aside —] ~ . —
185, 187 Ime] Q(u); I'me Q(c)
204 then?] ~ ,
207 ile] Q(u); Ile Q(c)
209 burnt.] Q(u); ~ ? Q(c)
222–223 hobby-|horse] hobbyhorse
223 towne to] to wneto
245 dangerous] dangerons
246 me —] ~ .

108

---

*Fig. 14e. Sample page of emendations of accidentals from Bowers'
Dekker.*

THE PLAYS AND
POEMS OF
Philip Massinger

EDITED BY
PHILIP EDWARDS
AND
COLIN GIBSON

VOLUME I

OXFORD
AT THE CLARENDON PRESS
1976

Fig. 15a *Title page: Volume I of Edwards and Gibson's edition of Massinger.*

I. ii. 43–73   *The Fatal Dowry*   23

Your Lordship will be pleasd to name the man,
Which you would haue your successor, and in me,
All promise to confirme it.
    Rochfort.   I embrace it,   45
As an assurance of their fauour to me,
And name my Lord *Nouall.*
    Du Croy.   The Court allows it.
    Rochfort. But there are suters waite heere, and their causes
May be of more necessity to be heard,
I therefore wish that mine may be defer'd,   50
And theirs haue hearing.
    Du Croy.   If your Lordship please
To take the place, we will proceed.
    Charmi.   The cause
We come to offer to your Lordships censure,
Is in it selfe so noble, that it needs not
Or Rhetorique in me that plead, or fauour   55
From your graue Lordships, to determine of it:
Since to the prayse of your impartiall iustice
(Which guilty, nay condemn'd men, dare not scandall)
Ciᵛ It will erect a trophy of your mercy
Which married to that Iustice—
    Nouall Senior.   Speake to the cause.   60
    Charmi. I will, my Lord: to say, the late dead Marshall
The father of this young Lord heere, my Clyent,
Hath done his Country great and faithfull seruice,
Might taske me of impertinence, to repeate
What your graue Lordships cannot but remember.   65
He in his life, became indebted to
These thriftie men, I will not wrong their credits,
By giuing them the attributes they now merit,
And fayling by the fortune of the warres,
Of meanes to free himselfe, from his ingagements,   70
He was arrested, and for want of bayle
Imprisond at their suite, and not long after
With losse of liberty ended his life.

50. I] *Gifford;* And *32*   56. it:] *Mason* (;) ; ~. *32*   60. Which] *Coxeter;*
With *32*   Iustice—] *Mason;* ~. *32*   64. impertinence, to repeate] *Coxeter;*
impertinence to repeate, *32*   65. remember.] *Gifford;* ~, *32*   66. became]
Mason; become *32*

Fig. 15b.   Sample page of text from Edwards and Gibson's Massinger.

APPENDIX I

RUNNING CORRECTIONS TO THE TEXT

The Fatal Dowry

I. i

      Actus] Act.
10   runne] ~,
14   deserue] 32²; deserne 32¹
17   Presidents] 32²; presidents 32¹
29   you] 32²; yon 32¹
33   dulnesse,] ~∧
36   *Charaloyes*] *Charloyes*
42   meriting] ~,
48   *Du Croye* 32²; *Dn* ~ 32¹
57   eyes] ~,
69   innocence] ~,
70   that,] ~∧
99   goodnesse!] ~?
108   this,] ~∧
116   corruption,] ~;
      friend;] ~,
133   too.] 32²; ~, 32¹
140   assurance] 32²; assurauce 32¹
150   lawlesse,] ~;
151   That] that
159   inheritance] ~,
161   and] &
166   Luxury] *Luxury*
171 SD. *Exeunt*] *Ex*:
173   sorrow] ~,
195   shelfe] ~,

I. ii

7   resigne,] ~∧
19   me] ~,
22   well] ~,
31   spent,] ~∧
90   boldnesse] bodldnesse
108   there,] ~∧
129   them,] ~;
134   soldyer,] ~:
146 SD. *Exeunt*] *Ex.*

171   *Charaloyes*] *Charloyes*
174   patrimony] patri mony
177   after] After
181   peace.] 32²; ~.; 32¹
182   liues] 32²; liue 32¹
187   from] frō
189   Sufficient] Sufficent
190   barre,] ~:
191   warre:] ~,
231   themselues] ~,
255 SD. *Exeunt*] *Exit*
      and] &
288 SD. *Exeunt*] *Ex.*
      and] &
289   Baumont!] ~.
293   *Charaloyes*] *Charloyes*

II. i

      Actus] Act.
10   'tis] 'Tis
14   old,] ~∧
28   inioy,] ~;
47 SD. speaks,] ~.
      weeping.] ~,
      Musique.] ~,
49   sighes,] ~;
70   hath,] ~.
74   What,] ~∧
83   pillars,] ~∧
89   Bayes,] ~∧
94   Damn'd!] ~,
      ha, ha, ha.] ~! ~, ~.
95   wee'ld] weel'd
97   birth,] ~∧
      rogues!] ~.
114   Curace,] ~∧
127   house.] ~,
128   inheritance,] ~.
144   Iuly,] ~;

8118045.5   B

Fig. 15c.   Sample page of an appendix listing "corrections" (i.e., emendations) to the text, including only those not recorded at the foot of the text itself (fig. 15b), from Edwards and Gibson's Massinger.

COMMENTARY

THE FATAL DOWRY

Cast

32 gives a list of the names of the characters only; the descriptions given here are based on Gifford, the first editor to supply them, but the order of *32*'s list has been retained. The 'Officers' vary in rank, from 'presidents' in Act I to bailiffs in Act V.

Act I

I. i. 1. *I may moue . . . your will*] 'I may make an application to the Court, in obedience to your will'.

9. *doe your parts*] do your part; cf. I. ii. 9, V. ii. 160.

19. *him selfe*] *32*'s 'your selfe' gives a most awkward change from third person to second person, followed in the next line by a return to the third person.

33. *This such a dulnesse*] 'this' for 'this is' can be paralleled, e.g. *Measure for Measure*, V. i. 131, 'this' a good Fryer' (Folio), and *King Lear*, IV. vi. 184, 'This a good block.' There is a strong pause before *This* which makes the rhythm sound.

36. *Charaloyes*] spelt *Charloyes* in *32*; see Introduction, p. 2.

37. *Marshall*] commander of the army, after the Duke of Burgundy.

37-8. *from whom he inherits . . . onely*] from the arguments of Arellius Fuscus in Seneca's *controversia*, which is the source of the play (see Introduction, p. 4): *Damnatus peculatus nihil aliud heredi suo reliquit quam se patrem.*

44-5 *satisfie . . . The summes*] The more usual construction would be 'of the sums', but *OED* remarks that the debt is occasionally found as a second object after 'satisfy'.

49. *Colonell*] three syllables, as it was usually spoken at this time, though on one or two occasions (e.g. III. i. 214) in this play it is slurred into two syllables.

70-1. *and in that, Assurance*] 'and in doing that (*flying to her succours*), having assurance'.

76. *sops*] for 'a sop to Cerberus', see Tilley, S 643; earliest usage, 1513.

87-9. *To drowne . . . against her*] 'to speak out against the oratory of a corrupt advocate and make him give back the money he took to oppose her'. A fee is returned by an outmanœuvred pleader in the next scene (220-4).

102 SD. *Enter . . . CREDITORS*] The stage-direction in *32* is crowded into the margin, beginning opposite ''Tis well', and editors have been puzzled, supposing the entry to follow that phrase. Gifford transferred ''Tis well' to Charalois; McIlwraith, leaving the words with Romont, thought they marked Romont's approval of a practice bow. But marginal entries are placed where they can conveniently be printed; ''Tis well' surely follows the entry and acknowledges Charalois' obeisance to the new arrivals.

Advocates leave the stage at line 139, and an entrance should be provided for them here. It is possible that the entrance had been struck out in the preparation of the prompt-book; the presence of the silent advocates adds nothing, and uses up actors.

Fig. 15d. Sample page of textual and explanatory commentary from Edwards and Gibson's Massinger.

Mardi

and

A Voyage Thither

HERMAN MELVILLE

NORTHWESTERN UNIVERSITY PRESS
and
THE NEWBERRY LIBRARY

Evanston and Chicago
1970

Fig. 16a   Title page of the Northwestern-Newberry edition of Melville's Mardi, *edited by Harrison Hayford, Hershel Parker, and G. Thomas Tanselle.*

Fig. 16b.   Copyright page from the Northwestern-Newberry Mardi, *with the CEAA seal.*

Chapter 75

Time and Temples

I N THE ORIENTAL Pilgrimage of the pious old Purchas, and in the
fine old folio Voyages of Hakluyt, Thevenot, Ramusio, and De Bry,
we read of many glorious old Asiatic temples, very long in erecting.
And veracious Gaudentio di Lucca hath a wondrous narration of the time
consumed in rearing that mighty three-hundred-and-sixty-five-pillared
Temple of the Year, somewhere beyond Libya; whereof, the columns did
signify days, and all round fronted upon concentric zones of palaces, cross-
cut by twelve grand avenues symbolizing the signs of the zodiac, all radia-
ting from the sun-dome in their midst. And in that wild eastern tale of his,
Marco Polo tells us, how the Great Mogul began him a pleasure-palace on
so imperial a scale, that his grandson had much ado to complete it.

But no matter for marveling all this: great towers take time to construct.
And so of all else.

And that which long endures full-fledged, must have long lain in the
germ. And duration is not of the future, but of the past; and eternity is
eternal, because it has been; and though a strong new monument be builded
to-day, it only is lasting because its blocks are old as the sun. It is not the
Pyramids that are ancient, but the eternal granite whereof they are made;
which had been equally ancient though yet in the quarry. For to make an
eternity, we must build with eternities; whence, the vanity of the cry for

228

Fig. 16c.   Sample page of text from the Northwestern-Newberry **Mardi.**

228.6   Gaudentio]   See note on 228.7.

228.7   -sixty-]   NN emends the A and E reading "three-hundred-and-seventy-five" to "three-hundred-and-sixty-five". Nathalia Wright called the editors' attention to this reading, pointing out that in Simon Berington's fictional *Memoirs of Sigr. Gaudentio di Lucca* (1737) the number of pillars in the "Temple of the Year," which is alluded to here, is appropriately 365. It is unlikely that in making the allusion Melville was not aware of the obvious point that the number of pillars corresponds to the number of days in the year and so wrote out the pointless number 375. Probably he saw the point and wrote out the proper number but in a way that induced a misreading by a copyist or compositor unaware of the point. Also corrected by NN is the A and E misspelling "Gaudentia" (228.6) for "Gaudentio", likewise on grounds of a probable misreading of Melville's manuscript.

248.2   *Donjalolo*]   The comma after "DONJALOLO" in A was removed in E; the change from "DONJALOLO" to "*Donjalolo*" is made in conformity with the styling of NN.

275.18–20   "The . . . hopes."]   This paragraph was not enclosed in quotation marks in A and E, but NN supplies the quotation marks since the comments are clearly the conclusion of Braid-Beard's speech.

281.34   above]   Both the A reading, retained by NN, and the E reading "about" make good sense in the context. As he "began over again" Yoomy either (as E has it) repeated the phrase "about ten hundred thousand moons" or (as A has it), having been challenged by Mohi the historian, he defiantly increased the time to "above ten hundred thousand moons". No ground exists for rejecting the copy-text reading.

298.5   them]   E repeats "stay-at-homes" in place of "them"; the change seems deliberately made to avoid the possible faulty reference of "them" to "travelers" rather than to "stay-at-homes". The change is not adopted by NN, however, since someone at Bentley's or even the compositor could have made it.

327.19   desire]   The E reading "require" somewhat strengthens Media's question, since in fact the old man does require, not merely desire, recompense. The change may be deliberate, not merely a compositorial misreading. Since, however, it cannot be taken as necessarily an authorial change, it is not adopted by NN.

368.1–2   enter many nations]   NN retains the A and E reading, assuming that the sense is merely that the speaker casually enters many nations, even as Mungo Park rested (or visited) in many African cots, and that no exact equivalence is intended between the number of nations and the number of cots (in which case "as" would be required after "enter").

Fig. 16d. Sample page of textual commentary from the Northwestern-Newberry edition of Mardi. *(A = American edition, E = English edition, NN = Northwestern-Newberry edition.)*

	NN Reading	Copy-text Reading
4.32	symptoms E	symptons
6.1	Kamschatka NN	Kamschatska
15.4	reminiscences E	reminiscenses
22.17	the crew E	thc crew
40.6	Caribbean NN	Carribean
43.4	jackknife NN	jacknife
55.4	on E	an
62.10	brakes NN	breaks
66.28	Annatoo!" E	~!∧
87.38	as E	of
*88.1	of NN	as
104.35	lunge NN	lounge
105.30	Crockett's NN	Crocket's
119.8	pump-brakes NN	pump-breaks
123.11	phosphorescence E	phosphoresence
147.9	philippic NN	phillipic
150.9	fish, we E	Fish, we
175.13	Archipelago. E	~∧
175.25	transmissible NN	transmissable
185.4	twelve.∧ E	~."
192.12	windrows NN	winrows
196.21	attendants. E	~,
203.26	itself. E	~,
210.12	us, E	~.
211.10	shall NN	Shall
212.13	Braid-Beard NN	Braid-beard
220.8	to the E	to tho
*228.6	Gaudentio NN	Gaudentia
*228.7	-sixty- NN	-seventy-
233.6	mouth E	month
246.21	nut. NN	~,
247.5	'Ah E	"~
247.5	fancy,' E	~,"

Fig. 16e. Sample page of the list of emendations in the Northwestern-Newberry edition of Mardi.

178.19	jet-black	333.28	forty-seven
179.5	scroll-prowed	335.6	water-course
185.13	bulkheads	336.26	forest-tree
189.25	whirlpool	344.11	to-day
191.38	demi-god	344.28	anaconda-like
197.34	high-spirited	344.34	many-limbed
200.23	paddle-blades	352.10	stopping-places
200.26	shark's-mouth	366.16	vineyards
201.5	arrow-flights	367.24	land-locked
203.15	To-day	367.31	sea-side
212.13	Braid-Beard	372.8	cocoa-nut
217.27	sea-cavern	372.16	red-barked
225.3	†overarched	372.16	†net-work
226.29	†sweet-scented	372.20	†mouth-piece
231.15	overlooking	372.35	pipe-bowl
232.2	overlapping	373.10	pipe-bowls
237.37	balsam-dropping	374.15	black-letter
240.2	torch-light	374.23	coffin-lid
240.5	sea-girt	376.4	berry-brown
240.8	golden-rinded	376.25	skull-bowl
243.13	woe-begone	379.35	†foot-prints
243.28	burial-place	380.13	†swordfish
246.11	under-breeding	385.14	midmost
246.12	Arva-root	385.33	worm-eaten
253.17	milk-white	387.13	undertaker
256.38	lordly-looking	396.2	market-place
268.1	moss-roses	406.33	semi-transparent
271.10	overstepped	416.21	foot-prints
282.37	star-fish	418.21	cocoa-nuts
282.39	swordfish	423.20	rose-balm
283.16	moonbeams	426.39	†foreordained
285.14	close-grappling	446.5	purple-robed
286.8	overstrained	446.20	guava-rind
287.19	merry-making	456.39	after-birth
288.28	nursery-talk	463.23	oftentimes
289.1	tiger-sharks	467.34	snow-drifts
290.23	circumnavigated	467.35	ice-bergs
295.23	cocoa-nut	479.12	†river-horse
297.20	Commonwealth's	482.6	lord-mayor
330.9	palm-nuts	482.11	dragon-beaked
330.19	†halberd-shaped	482.18	sea-king
332.22	demi-gods	489.27	sword-hilt

Fig. 16f. Sample page of the report of line-end hyphenations from the Northwestern-Newberry edition of Mardi. *The lists presents the editors' treatment of words hyphenated in the copy-text. (Daggered entries are words coincidentally hyphenated in the copy-text and Northwestern-Newberry edition and are recorded according to how the editors would have treated them had they not been broken at the end of a line.)*

SUBSTANTIVE VARIANTS		719
101.17–18	blue boundless A	boundless blue E
105.10	spiteful A	[*omitted*] E
106.18	could A	[*omitted*] E
106.18	see A	saw E
108.6	then A	[*omitted*] E
123.3	to A	by E
123.39	upon A	on E
125.16	And at A	At E
125.18	sedulously kept A	kept sedulously E
127.3	in A	[*omitted*] E
136.14	cheek A	cheeks E
144.12	as A	a E
150.32	the A	a E
153.14	was A	must have been E
157.14	would A	should E
176.37	one A	[*omitted*] E
192.26	over A	our E
202.22	loyal A	royal E
203.23	and A	an E
211.16	for A	that, for E
211.17	but A	[*omitted*] E
211.17	a A	a mere E
228.7	that A	the E
233.6	mouth NN month A	mouth E
239.4	of the A	of E
246.13	then A	just then E
265.4	pass A	passed E
270.18	And . . . Mohi. A	[*omitted*] E
280.11	he A	the E
281.34	above A	about E
285.9	Kings A	King's E
289.4	a A	an E
297.9	swab A	to swab E

Fig. 16g.   Sample page of the list of substantive variants between the American edition (copy-text) and English edition, from the Northwestern-Newberry edition of Mardi.

Appendix on Textual Notation

Although scholarly publishers and scholarly editors have adopted various forms of textual notation over the years, the generally accepted style is that enunciated by R. B. McKerrow in his *Prolegomena for the Oxford Shakespeare* (Oxford: Clarendon, 1939). It is a method adaptable for either horizontal or vertical variants as well as for the apparatus of the finished edition.

Its basic principle is that the lemmatic reading—that reading found to the left-hand side of the open bracket—is always the reading of the base text (in working collational notes) or of the edited text (in the textual notes in an edition's apparatus) and that the readings to the right-hand side are the stemmatic readings. Thus simple variation is recorded as:

231. George] Iohn

"231" is the exact line reference to either the base text or edited text and can, of course, take whatever form is most convenient and conventional for recording an exact line location. For example, in plays it has been conventional to make reference by act, scene, and line: II.iii.231; in long subdivided poems, like *The Faerie Queene*, by book, canto, stanza, and line: III.i.13.6. Of course, for shorter poems a line number alone is sufficient. In recent years, however, editors have adopted the practice of through-line-numbering for all but the longest poems, ignoring act, scene, book, canto, stanza, and other divisions and assigning each line a sequential line number. For prose works the problem is slightly more difficult because line numbers are not constant, the lines varying from edition to edition in length and, therefore, in the material they contain. A common practice is to make reference by page and line number of the base text or edited text:

G1r.35, or 123.41.

In the example above "George" is the reading in line 231 of the base or edited text and "Iohn" the variant reading in another text. To identify the other text, a siglum must be added:

    231.   George] Iohn *B3*

"*B3*" is the identifying symbol for that particular copy or edition which contains that reading.

    A swung dash (∼) indicates that portions of the stemmatic reading agree with the lemmatic readings:

    231.   ran] ∼, *B3*

An inferior caret indicates where the stemmatic readings lack punctuation found in the lemmatic reading:

    231.   ran,] ∼ˌ *B3*

When the stemmatic readings lack material, it is indicated thus:

    231.   and Harry] *om. B3*

In cases where the lemmatic readings omit material or lack punctuation, the information is recorded thus:

    231.   Betty] ∼ and Sally *B3*
    231.   sat] ∼, *B3*

Placing these symbols (ˏ , ∼, or *om*) to the left of the bracket would at least imply that the base or edited text contained those marks in it.

    If no accidental or substantive variants save lineation occur, lineation changes in poetry are indicated thus:

    232–3.   They … down / Now … grown] They … dew / Help … hew *B3*

If other variants occur, the stemmatic readings, with line division indication, must be fully written out. Of course, in prose no record is kept of lineation, although a record should be kept of line-end hyphenation for all those words that might be hyphenated even if they appeared in mid-line.

    If several texts share a variant reading their sigla are added to the note:

    231.   George] Iohn *B3, B4, B8*

If there are several readings:

    231.   George] Iohn *B3, B4, B8*; John *B5, B6*

It is assumed that all sigla not shown as disagreeing with the lemmatic reading agree with it. If all subsequent texts share a variant, the plus sign is employed:

231.   and Harry] *om. B3* +

These are the conventions and forms for recording variation. In the edited text it will also be necessary to record emendations in the copy-text. Again, the lemmatic reading is that found in the edited text, so that if the editor decides that the authoritative reading is different from that found in the copy-text, he or she must record that fact.

231.   Iohn] *B5*; George *B1, B2, B7*; John *B3, B4, B8*

This note shows that the reading "Iohn" does not come from the copy-text, *B1*, that its earliest appearance is in *B5*, and that all other texts except *B6* have different readings. There is no need to record *B6* since we assume texts not found in the stemmatic readings agree with the lemmatic readings. If the editor must emend on his or her own authority the following form of note suffices:

231.   Ralph] George *B1, B2, B7*; John *B3, B4, B8*; Iohn *B5, B6*

Some editors place the siglum of their own edition to the right of the bracket in such an instance.

   Although readers of this book will find many variations from this notational system, it has proved itself the clearest, most useful, and most widely accepted of all methods of recording variations and emendations.

Reference Bibliography

INTRODUCTION AND DEFINITIONS

Definitions of bibliography and its subdivisions appear in Fredson Bowers' "Bibliography, Pure Bibliography, and Literary Studies" and in the other five essays gathered under the heading "The Bibliographical Way" in his *Essays in Bibliography, Text, and Editing* (Charlottesville: Univ. Press of Virginia, 1975), pp. 3–108. Other important essays in definition are Lloyd Hibberd's "Physical and Reference Bibliography," *Library*, 5th ser., 20 (1965), 124–34; Rolf Du Rietz's "What Is Bibliography?" *Text*, 1 (1974), 6–40; G. Thomas Tanselle's "Bibliography and Science" (1974) and "Descriptive Bibliography and Library Cataloguing" (1977), collected in his *Selected Studies in Bibliography* (Charlottesville: Univ. Press of Virginia, 1979), pp. 1–92; and Ross Atkinson's "An Application of Semiotics to the Definition of Bibliography," *SB*, 33 (1980), 54–73. A history of the term "bibliography," especially its European usage from the seventeenth through twentieth centuries, is provided by Rudolf Blum's *Bibliographia: An Inquiry into Its Definition and Designations* (1969), trans. Mathilde V. Rovelstad (Chicago: American Library Assn.; Kent: Dawson, 1980).

Among the basic means of access to bibliographical and textual studies are the *Dictionary Catalogue of the History of Printing from the John M. Wing Foundation in the Newberry Library*, 9 vols. (Boston: Hall, 1961, 1970); the volumes of T. H. Howard-Hill's *Index to British Literary Bibliography* (Oxford: Clarendon, 1969–), including *Bibliography of British Literary Bibliographies* (1969), *Shakespearian Bibliography and Textual Criticism* (1971), and *British Bibliography and Textual Criticism* (2 vols., 1979); and Robin Myers' *The British Book Trade from Caxton to the Present* (London: Deutsch, 1973). For British topics, these should be supplemented, of course, by the *New Cambridge Bibliography of English Literature*, 5 vols. (Cambridge: Cambridge Univ. Press, 1969–77); for American topics, by the bibliography volume of the *Literary History of the United States*, ed. Robert E. Spiller et al., 4th ed. (New York: Macmillan, 1974), and by G. Thomas Tanselle's *Guide to the Study of United States Imprints*, 2 vols. (Cambridge: Harvard Univ. Press, 1971).

From 1950 through 1974 the annual *Studies in Bibliography* published check-lists of bibliographical scholarship. The lists for 1949–55 were collected and indexed in *SB*, 10 (1957); those for 1956–62, in *Selective Check Lists of Bibliographical Scholarship*, ser. B (Charlottesville: Univ. Press of Virginia, 1966). Among the current serial bibliographies that are especially useful are the *Annual Bibliography of the History of the Printed Book* (1973–   ), the *MLA International Bibliography* (1922–   ), and the MHRA *Annual Bibliography of English Language and Literature* (1921–   ). The most important periodicals in the field are *The Library, Studies in Bibliography (SB)*, and *Papers of the Bibliographical Society of America (PBSA)*. A survey of such journals from past and present appears in G. Thomas Tanselle's "The Periodical Literature of English and American Bibliography," *SB* 26 (1973), 167–91.

ANALYTICAL BIBLIOGRAPHY

There is no standard, comprehensive treatment of analytical bibliography. Ronald B. McKerrow's *An Introduction to Bibliography for Literary Students* (Oxford: Clarendon, 1928), though much of it is outdated, remains a valuable primer, especially when combined with Philip Gaskell's *A New Introduction to Bibliography* (Oxford: Oxford Univ. Press, 1972), which emphasizes the materials and methods of printing and contains lists of primary and secondary works in historical bibliography, works essential for analytical bibliography. Published and unpublished items available for the historical and analytical bibliography of the sixteenth through eighteenth centuries are surveyed by Philip Rider, Paul Werstine, William P. Williams, and O M Brack, Jr., in "Research Opportunities in the Early English Book Trade," *Analytical & Enumerative Bibliography*, 3 (1979), 165–200. G. Thomas Tanselle surveys English and American copyright records in "Copyright Records and the Bibliographer," *SB*, 22 (1969), 77–124, reprinted in his *Selected Studies in Bibliography* (Charlottesville: Univ. Press of Virginia), pp. 93–138. An important dictionary of printing and publishing (and thus bibliographical) vocabulary is Geoffrey A. Glaister's *A Glossary of the Book* (London: Allen & Unwin, 1960), published in the United States as *An Encyclopedia of the Book* (Cleveland: World, 1960) and in a second edition as *Glaister's Glossary of the Book* (Berkeley: Univ. of California Press, 1979).

Because there is no entirely satisfactory introduction, one must learn analytical bibliography by consulting studies that focus on a particular type of evidence or on its application to a particular problem. Foremost among these studies is Charlton Hinman's *The Printing and Proof-Reading of the First Folio of Shakespeare*, 2 vols. (Oxford: Clarendon, 1963), a model of analytical technique. For its use of watermark evidence, a similar model is A. H. Stevenson's *The Problem of the Missale Speciale* (London: Bibliographical Soc., 1967). And for both paper and typographical evidence, there are J. W. Carter and H. G. Pollard's *An Enquiry into the Nature of Certain Nineteenth-Century Pamphlets*

(London: Constable, 1934; augmented ed., 1983) and Peter W. M. Blayney's *Nicholas Okes and the First Quarto*, Vol. I of *The Texts of* King Lear *and Their Origins* (Cambridge: Cambridge Univ. Press, 1982). As these titles suggest, many developments in analytical bibliography are contained in studies of particular books—studies that are listed in the basic bibliographical resources cited above. To list any here is to slight a great many others; nonetheless, the following examples will indicate the nature and diversity of such studies: D. F. McKenzie, " 'Indenting the Stick' in the First Quarto of *King Lear* (1608)," *PBSA*, 67 (1973), 125–30; George R. Price, "The Printing of *Love's Labour's Lost* (1598)," *PBSA*, 72 (1978), 405–34; W. Speed Hill, "Casting Off Copy and the Composition of Hooker's Book V," *SB*, 33 (1980), 144–61; William B. Todd, "Concurrent Printing: An Analysis of Dodsley's *Collection of Poems by Several Hands*," *PBSA*, 46 (1952), 45–57; Joseph Katz, "Analytical Bibliography and Literary History: The Writing and Printing of *Wieland*," *Proof*, 1 (1971), 8–34; Peter L. Shillingsburg, "The Printing, Proof-Reading, and Publishing of Thackeray's *Vanity Fair*: The First Edition," *SB*, 34 (1981), 118–45; Matthew Bruccoli and Charles A. Rheault, Jr., "Imposition Figures and Plate Gangs in *The Rescue*," *SB*, 14 (1961), 258–62; William B. Todd, "The White House Transcripts," *PBSA*, 68 (1974), 267–96.

Other studies focus on a particular kind of evidence or method of analysis, as in these examples: Richard N. Schwab et al., "Cyclotron Analysis of the Ink in the Forty-Two Line Bible," *PBSA*, 77 (1983), 285–315; Allan Stevenson, "Paper as Bibliographical Evidence," *Library*, 5th ser., 17 (1962), 197–212; Stephen Spector, "Symmetry in Watermark Sequences," *SB*, 31 (1978), 162–78; Curt Buhler, "The Margins in Mediaeval Books," *PBSA*, 40 (1946), 34–42; William H. Bond, "Casting Off Copy by Elizabethan Printers," *PBSA*, 42 (1948), 281–91; R. A. Sayce, "Compositorial Practices and the Localization of Printed Books, 1530–1800," *Library*, 5th ser., 21 (1966), 1–45; Robert K. Turner, Jr., "Reappearing Types as Bibliographical Evidence," *SB*, 19 (1966), 198–209; Fredson Bowers, "Bibliographical Evidence from the Printer's Measure," *SB*, 2 (1949–50), 153–67; George Walton Williams, "Setting by Formes in Quarto Printing," *SB*, 11 (1958), 39–53; Kenneth Povey, "Working to Rule, 1600–1800: A Study of Pressmen's Practice," *Library*, 20 (1965), 13–54; William H. Bond, "Imposition by Half-Sheets," *Library*, 4th ser., 22 (1941–42), 163–67; Bowers, "Running-Title Evidence for Determining Half-Sheet Imposition," *SB*, 1 (1948–49), 199–202; Povey, "On the Diagnosis of Half-Sheet Imposition," *Library*, 5th ser., 11 (1956), 268–72; Oliver L. Steele, "Half-Sheet Imposition of Eight-Leaf Quires in Formes of Thirty-Two and Sixty-Four Pages," *SB*, 15 (1962), 274–78; Povey, "Variant Formes in Elizabethan Printing," *Library*, 5th ser., 10 (1955), 41–48; Povey, "The Optical Identification of First Formes," *SB*, 13 (1960), 189–90; Ernest W. Sullivan II, "Marginal Rules as Evidence," *SB*, 30 (1977), 171–80; D. F. Foxon, "On Printing 'At One Pull' and Distinguishing Impressions by Point-Holes," *Library*, 5th ser., 11 (1956), 284–85; Peter L. Shillingsburg, "Register Measurement as a Method of Detecting Hidden Printings," *PBSA*, 73 (1979), 484–88; William B. Todd, "Observations on the Incidence and Interpretation of Press Figures," *SB*, 3 (1950–51), 171–205; Povey, "A Century of Press Figures," *Library*, 5th ser., 14 (1959), 251–73; G. Thomas Tanselle, "Press Figures in America: Some Preliminary Observations," *SB*, 19 (1966), 123–60; Todd, "Recurrent Printing," *SB*, 12 (1959), 189–98; Craig Abbott, "Offset Slur as Bibliographical Evidence," *PBSA*, 70 (1976), 538–41; Matthew J. Bruccoli, "A Mirror for Bibliographers: Duplicate Plates in Modern Printing," *PBSA*, 54 (1960), 83–88; Todd, "On the Use of Advertisements in Bibliographical Studies," *Library*, 5th ser., 8 (1953), 174–87. And, of course, descriptive bibliographies and textual studies (including critical editions) should be consulted for their application of analytical bibliography.

Finally, there are general and theoretical treatments of analytical bibliography. Fredson Bowers' *Bibliography and Textual Criticism* (Oxford: Clarendon, 1964), for example, deals with its relation to textual criticism and with its method of reasoning. D. F. McKenzie's "Printers of the Mind: Some Notes on Bibliographical Theories and Printing-House Practices," *SB*, 22 (1969), 1–75, as well as his "Stretching a Point: Or, The Case of the Spaced-Out Comps," *SB*, 37 (1984), 106–21, questions assumptions about the normality and regularity of printing practices. In part an answer to McKenzie is G. Thomas Tanselle's "Bibliography and Science," *SB*, 27 (1974), 55–89. In "The Selection and Presentation of Bibliographical Evidence," *Analytical & Enumerative Bibliography*, 1 (1977), 101–36, Peter Davison deals with the same question and offers some practical suggestions in using and reporting bibliographical evidence.

DESCRIPTIVE BIBLIOGRAPHY

The standard treatment is Fredson Bowers' *Principles of Bibliographical Description* (Princeton: Princeton Univ. Press, 1949; rpt. New York: Russell, 1962). More extended treatment of the degressive principle, the purposes of description, and the need to adjust description to the materials examined is offered by Bowers in "Purposes of Descriptive Bibliography, with Some Remarks on Methods" (1952) and "Bibliography Revisited" (1969), both reprinted in his *Essays in Bibliography, Text, and Editing* (Charlottesville: Univ. Press of Virginia), pp. 111–34, 151–95. G. Thomas Tanselle deals with the problem of degree of accuracy in "Tolerances in Bibliographical Description," *Library*, 5th ser., 23 (1968), 1–12; with ideal copy in "The Concept of Ideal Copy," *SB*, 33 (1980), 18–53; and with the distinction between describing a single copy and describing ideal copy in "Descriptive Bibliography and Library Cataloguing," *SB*, 30 (1977), 1–56. In a number of articles, Tanselle has proposed elaborations, refinements, and modifications of Bowers' *Principles*: "A System of Color Identification for Bibliographical Description" (1967); "The Bibliographical Description of Patterns" (1970); "The Bibliographical Description of Paper" (1971); "The Identification of Type Faces in Bibliographical Description," *Library*, 5th ser., 23 (1968), 1–12; "The Use of Type Damage as Evidence in Bibliographical

Description," *Library*, 5th ser., 23 (1968), 328–51; "Book-Jackets, Blurbs, and Bibliographers," *Library*, 5th ser, 26 (1971), 91–134; and "The Description of Non-Letterpress Material in Books," *SB*, 35 (1982), 1–42. The first three of these are reprinted from *SB* in his *Selected Studies in Bibliography* (Charlottesville: Univ. Press of Virginia), pp. 139–243. David F. Foxon's *Thoughts on the History and Future of Bibliographical Description* (Berkeley: Univ. of California, 1970) is concerned largely with questioning the value of quasifacsimile transcriptions of title pages. Bibliographical taxonomy, treated at length in Bowers' *Principles*, has also been discussed in James B. Meriwether and Joseph Katz's "A Redefinition of 'Issue,' " *Proof*, 2 (1972), 61–70; in Tanselle's "The Bibliographical Concept of 'Issue' and 'State,' " *PBSA*, 69 (1975), 17–66, and his "The Arrangement of Descriptive Bibliographies," *SB*, 37 (1984), 1–38; and in James L. W. West III's "The Bibliographical Concept of Plating," *SB*, 36 (1983), 252–66.

Of course, the various theoretical and methodological approaches are applied and tested in bibliographies. Thus a person interested in descriptive bibliography should consult actual bibliographies and examine their successes and failures. The following are a few notable examples: Warner Barnes, *A Bibliography of Elizabeth Barrett Browning* (Austin: Humanities Research Center; Waco: Armstrong Browning Library, 1967); Jacob Blanck, *Bibliography of American Literature* (New Haven: Yale Univ. Press, 1955–   ); B. C. Bloomfield and Edward Mendelson, *W. H. Auden: A Bibliography, 1924–1969*, 2nd ed. (Charlottesville: Univ. Press of Virginia, 1972); Edwin Bowden, *James Thurber: A Bibliography* (Columbus: Ohio State Univ. Press, 1968); Matthew J. Bruccoli, *F. Scott Fitzgerald: A Descriptive Bibliography* (Pittsburgh: Univ. of Pittsburgh Press, 1972); C. E. Frazer Clark, Jr., *Nathaniel Hawthorne: A Descriptive Bibliography* (Pittsburgh: Univ. of Pittsburgh Press, 1978); Philip Gaskell, *A Bibliography of the Foulis Press* (London: Hart-Davis, 1964); W. W. Greg, *A Bibliography of the English Printed Drama to the Restoration*, 4 vols. (London: Bibliographical Soc., 1939–59); Geoffrey Keynes, *A Bibliography of George Berkeley* (Oxford: Clarendon, 1976); D. F. McKenzie, *Cambridge University Press, 1696–1712: A Bibliographical Survey* (Cambridge: Cambridge Univ. Press, 1966), vol. 1, app. 1; Joel Myerson, *Ralph Waldo Emerson: A Descriptive Bibliography* (Pittsburgh: Univ. of Pittsburgh Press, 1982); William B. Todd, *A Bibliography of Edmund Burke* (London: Hart-Davis, 1964); James L. W. West III, *William Styron: A Descriptive Bibliography* (Boston: Hall, 1977).

TEXTUAL CRITICISM

Two introductions to textual criticism, especially its editorial aspect, are Fredson Bowers' "Textual Criticism," in *The Aims and Methods of Scholarship in Modern Languages and Literatures*, ed. James Thorpe (New York: MLA, 1963), pp. 23–42, and G. Thomas Tanselle's "Textual Scholarship," in *Introduction to Scholarship in Modern Languages and Literatures*, ed. Joseph Gibaldi (New York: MLA, 1981) pp. 29–52. In *From Writer to Reader: Studies in Editorial Method* (Oxford: Clarendon, 1978) Philip Gaskell provides examples of textual histories and the editorial problems they present. The relationship between textual criticism and other fields is explored in Hershel Parker's "The 'New Scholarship': Textual Evidence and Its Implications for Criticism, Literary Theory, and Aesthetics," *Studies in American Fiction*, 9 (1981), 181–97; Jerome J. McGann's "The Text, the Poem, and the Problem of Historical Method," *New Literary History*, 12 (1981), 269–88; James Thorpe's "The Aesthetics of Textual Criticism" (1965), reprinted in his *Principles of Textual Criticism* (San Marino: Huntington Library, 1972), pp. 3–49; and Morse Peckham's "Reflections on the Foundations of Modern Textual Editing," *Proof*, 1 (1971), 122–55. The role of analytical bibliography and literary criticism is discussed in Bowers' *Bibliography and Textual Criticism* (Oxford: Clarendon, 1964) and *Textual and Literary Criticism* (Cambridge: Cambridge Univ. Press, 1959) and in Tanselle's "Textual Study and Literary Judgment," *PBSA*, 65 (1971), 109–22. An invaluable survey of scholarship on textual criticism, especially as it relates to editing, is contained in "The Center for Scholarly Editions: An Introductory Statement," *PMLA*, 92 (1977), 583–97, reprinted as a pamphlet (New York: MLA, 1977).

Among the many works on the study and editing of classical texts (and other texts with long manuscript traditions) are Paul Maas's *Textual Criticism*, trans. Barbara Flower (Oxford: Clarendon, 1958); Martin L. West's *Textual Criticism and Editorial Technique* (Stuttgart: Teubner, 1973); W. W. Greg's *The Calculus of Variants* (Oxford: Clarendon, 1927); Vinton Dearing's *Principles and Practice of Textual Analysis* (Berkeley: Univ. of California Press, 1974); and Charles Moorman's *Editing the Middle English Manuscript* (Jackson: Univ. Press of Mississippi, 1975). A review of recent developments, primarily in classical textual studies, may be found in Georg Luck's "Textual Criticism Today," *American Journal of Philology*, 102 (1981), 164–94. And in "Classical, Biblical, and Medieval Textual Criticism and Modern Editing," *SB*, 36 (1983), 21–68, Tanselle explores the relations between the editing of classical and modern texts. A thorough survey of documentary editing is provided by Tanselle in "The Editing of Historical Documents," *SB*, 31 (1978), 1–56, reprinted in his *Selected Studies in Bibliography* (Charlottesville: Univ. Press of Virginia, 1979), pp. 451–506. In "A New Approach to the Critical Constitution of Literary Texts," *SB*, 28 (1975), 231–64, Hans Zeller explains the rationale and methods of historical-critical editing.

A seminal document for modern critical editing is W. W. Greg's "The Rationale of Copy-Text," *SB*, 3 (1950–51), 19–36, reprinted in his *Collected Papers*, ed. J. C. Maxwell (Oxford: Clarendon, 1966), pp. 374–91. Most recent controversy in textual criticism has centered on the problem of copy-text and such related matters as authorial intention and the distinction between accidentals and substantives. As a pioneer in the application of Greg's rationale to both Renaissance and post-Renaissance texts, Fredson Bowers has been a key figure in the debate. Some of his most important contributions to it are reprinted in his *Essays in Bibliography, Text, and Editing* (Charlottesville: Univ. Press of Virginia, 1975); to them may be added "Scholarship and Editing," *PBSA*, 70 (1976), 161–88, and "Greg's 'Rationale of Copy-Text' Revisited," *SB*, 31 (1981), 90–161. The manual of the Center for Editions of American Authors—*Statement of Editorial Principles and Procedures*, rev. ed. (New York: MLA, 1972)—makes use of Greg's rationale in its outline of recommended methods. Among those taking exception to Greg's rationale are Paul Baender in "The Meaning of Copy-Text," *SB*, 22 (1969), 311–18, and Vinton A. Dearing in "Concepts of Copy-Text Old and New," *Library*, 5th ser., 28 (1973), 281–93. Tanselle has summarized and clarified the debate in "Greg's Theory of Copy-Text and the Editing of American Literature," *SB*, 28 (1975), 167–229 and has done the same for the related problem of intention in "The Editorial Problem of Final Authorial Intention," *SB*, 29 (1976), 167–211. (Both essays are reprinted in his *Selected Studies*, pp. 245–307, 309–53.) These and other matters are also considered in his "Recent Editorial Discussion and the Central Questions of Editing," *SB*, 34 (1981), 23–65, and in Peter L. Shillingsburg's "Key Issues in Editorial Theory," *Analytical & Enumerative Bibliography*, 6 (1982), 3–16. In *A Critique of Modern Textual Criticism* (Chicago: Univ. of Chicago Press, 1983), Jerome J. McGann questions final authorial intention and copy-text as strategies that neglect "the collaborative or social nature of literary production" (p. 125).

Many of the studies already cited treat the question of modernization of texts. Others may be added: Hershel Parker's "Regularizing Accidentals: The Latest Form of Infidelity," *Proof*, 3 (1973), 1–20; Ronald B. McKerrow's *Prolegomena for the Oxford Shakespeare: A Study in Editorial Method* (Oxford: Clarendon, 1939); and Stanley Wells's *Modernizing Shakespeare's Spelling* (Oxford: Clarendon, 1979). A thoughtful and instructive debate focusing on the critical implications of modernizing Shakespeare's sonnet 129 may be followed in Robert Graves and Laura Riding's essay "A Study in Original Punctuation and Spelling," revised from its 1927 appearance in their *Survey of Modernist Poetry* and collected in Graves's *The Common Asphodel* (London: Hamilton, 1949), pp. 84–95; in Stephen Booth's moderately modernized edition *Shakespeare's Sonnets* (New Haven: Yale Univ. Press, 1980), pp. 447–52; and then in Thomas M. Greene's "Anti-Hermeneutics: The Case of Shakespeare's Sonnet 129," in *Poetic Traditions of the English Renaissance*, ed. Maynard Mack and George deForest Lord (New Haven: Yale Univ. Press, 1982), pp. 142–61.

Several collections reprint some of the essays mentioned above or present other valuable essays on matters practical and theoretical: O M Brack, Jr., and Warner Barnes, eds., *Bibliography and Textual Criticism: English and American Literature, 1700 to the Present* (Chicago: Univ. of Chicago Press, 1969); Ronald Gottesman and Scott Bennett, eds., *Art and Error: Modern Textual*

Editing (Bloomington: Indiana Univ. Press, 1970); Warner Barnes and James T. Cox, eds., "Textual Studies in the Novel," a special issue of *Studies in the Novel*, 7 (1975), 317–471; and the series of volumes from the Editorial Conference, University of Toronto (1966–　).

A procedure for collation is briefly described in the CEAA *Statement of Editorial Principles and Procedures*. In "A Sampling Theory for Bibliographical Research," *Library*, 5th ser., 27 (1972), 310–19, David Shaw applies statistical methods to the problem of determining the number of copies that should be collated. Charlton Hinman describes his collating machine in "Mechanized Collation at the Houghton Library," *Harvard Library Bulletin*, 9 (1955), 132–34; and Gordon Lindstrand describes his in "Mechanized Textual Collation and Recent Designs," *SB*, 24 (1971), 204–14. In connection with these articles, one should consult George Guffey's "Standardization of Photographic Reproductions for Mechanical Collation," *PBSA*, 62 (1968), 237–40. The use of computers is surveyed in Robert L. Oakman's *Computer Methods for Literary Research* (Columbia: Univ. of South Carolina Press, 1980) and A. J. Aitken, R. W. Bailey, and N. Hamilton-Smith's *The Computer and Literary Studies* (Edinburgh: Univ. of Edinburgh Press, 1973).

McKerrow's *Prolegomena for the Oxford Shakespeare* presents a method for recording textual variants in an editorial apparatus. A more recent discussion is Tanselle's "Some Principles for Editorial Apparatus" (1972), in his *Selected Studies*, pp. 403–50. Both genetic and descriptive systems for recording manuscript variants are described in Bowers' "Transcription of Manuscripts: The Record of Variants," *SB*, 29 (1976), 212–64.

Finally, as examples of editorial method, scholarly editions of various kinds can be consulted. Notable are Fredson Bowers' editions of Thomas Dekker, Beaumont and Fletcher, Dryden, Fielding, and Marlowe, and the editions completed under the supervision or guidance of the Center for Editions of American Authors (1964–76) and the Center for Scholarly Editions (1976–　): for example, of Crane, Dewey, Emerson, Hawthorne, Howells, Irving, Melville, Thoreau, and Twain. These and other editions are listed in the CSE introductory statement. Also of note are the Folger Library edition of the works of Richard Hooker under the general editorship of W. Speed Hill and the Oxford Standard Editions such as William Ringler's edition of Sidney's poetry and Philip Edwards and Colin Gibson's edition of the plays and poems of Philip Massinger.

Notes

[1] *Shakespeare: Select Bibliographical Guides* (Oxford: Oxford Univ. Press, 1973), p. 13.

[2] Wilson's attack on the CEAA appeared in the *New York Review of Books*, 26 Sept. (pp. 7–10) and 10 Oct. 1968 (pp. 6, 8, 10, 12, 14), and was reprinted as *The Fruits of the MLA* (New York: New York Review, 1968). The CEAA responded in *Professional Standards and American Editions* (New York: MLA, 1969). The debate is surveyed by G. Thomas Tanselle in "Greg's Theory of Copy-Text and the Editing of American Literature," *SB*, 28 (1975), 167–229, reprinted in his *Selected Studies in Bibliography* (Charlottesville: Univ. Press of Virginia, 1979), pp. 245–307.

[3] Leon Edel, "The Text of *The Ambassadors*," *Harvard Library Bulletin*, 14 (1960), 453–60; Walter F. Staton, Jr., and W. E. Simeone, eds., *A Critical Edition of Sir Richard Fanshawe's 1647 Translation of Giovanni Battista Guarini's* Il Pastor Fido (Oxford: Clarendon 1964), p. 14.

[4] Febvre and Martin's study is available in English as *The Coming of the Book: The Impact of Printing, 1450–1800*, trans. David Gerard, ed. Geoffrey Nowell-Smith and David Wootton (Atlantic Highlands, N.J.: Humanities Press, 1976). Two other recent studies in the history of the book are Elizabeth L. Eisenstein's *The Printing Press as an Agent of Change* (Cambridge: Cambridge Univ. Press, 1979) and Robert Darnton's *The Business of Enlightenment: A Publishing History of the* Encyclopédie, *1775–1800* (Cambridge, Mass.: Belknap–Harvard Univ. Press, 1979).

[5] For studies of Davies' text see Robert Krueger, ed., *The Poems of Sir John Davies* (Oxford: Clarendon, 1975), and Charles B. Taylor, "A Critical Old Spelling Edition of Sir John Davies' *Nosce Teipsum*," Diss. Northern Illinois Univ. 1971.

[6] In a lecture at the University of Kansas on 14 Nov. 1958, published as *The Bibliographical Way* (Lawrence: Univ. of Kansas Libraries, 1959), p. 18; rpt. in his *Essays in Bibliography, Text, and Editing* (Charlottesville: Univ. Press of Virginia, 1975).

[7] Fredson Bowers, *Bibliography and Textual Criticism* (Oxford: Clarendon, 1964); D. F. McKenzie, "Printers of the Mind: Some Notes on Bibliographical Theories and Printing-House Practices," *SB*, 22 (1969), 1–75.

⁸ B. L. Browning, *Analysis of Paper*, 2nd ed. (New York: Marcel Dekker, 1977), pp. 335–36.

⁹ *An Enquiry into the Nature of Certain Nineteenth-Century Pamphlets* (London: Constable, 1934).

¹⁰ J. S. G. Simmons, "The Leningrad Method of Watermark Reproduction," *Book Collector*, 10 (1961), 329–30, and his "The Delft Method of Watermark Reproduction," *Book Collector*, 18 (1969), 514–15; also Warner Barnes, "Film Experimentation in Beta-Radiography," *Direction Line*, No. 1 (1975), pp. 3–4.

¹¹ W. W. Greg, "On Certain False Dates in Shakesperian Quartos," *Library*, 2nd ser., 9 (1908), 113–31, 381–409; A. W. Pollard, *Shakespeare Folios and Quartos: A Study in the Bibliography of Shakespeare's Plays, 1594–1685* (London: Methuen, 1909); and William J. Neidig, "The Shakespeare Quartos of 1619," *Modern Philology*, 8 (1910), 145–63.

¹² Charmian Poe, "Byron and Byroniana at Northern Illinois University: A Descriptive Catalogue," Diss. Northern Illinois Univ. 1980.

¹³ "Compositorial Practices and the Localization of Printed Books, 1530–1800," *Library*, 5th ser., 21 (1966), 1–45.

¹⁴ "Elizabethan Proofing" (1948), in his *Essays in Bibliography*, pp. 240–53.

¹⁵ Peter L. Shillingsburg, "Detecting the Use of Stereotype Plates," *Editorial Quarterly*, No. 1 (1975), pp. 2–3

¹⁶ See Bowers' "Was There a Lost 1593 Edition of Marlowe's *Edward II*?," *SB*, 25 (1972), 143–48, and his textual introduction to *The Complete Works of Christopher Marlowe*, 2nd ed. (Cambridge: Cambridge Univ. Press, 1981), II, 3–12.

¹⁷ See Vol. I of *The Centenary Edition of the Works of Nathaniel Hawthorne*, ed. William Charvat et al. (Columbus: Ohio State Univ. Press, 1962), especially the textual introduction by Fredson Bowers, pp. xlix–lxv. See also C. E. Frazer Clark, Jr., *Nathaniel Hawthorne: A Descriptive Bibliography* (Pittsburgh: Univ. of Pittsburgh Press, 1978), pp. 141–48.

¹⁸ Bowers makes this point in "Bibliography Revisited," *Library*, 5th ser., 24 (1969), 84–128; rpt. in his *Essays in Bibliography*, pp. 175–76.

¹⁹ James L. W. West III, *William Styron: A Descriptive Bibliography* (Boston: Hall, 1977), pp. 94–106.

²⁰ Madan, "Degressive Bibliography: A Memorandum," *Transactions of the Bibliographical Society*, 9 (1906–08), 53–65. The principle is discussed in Bowers' "Purposes of Descriptive Bibliography with Some Remarks on Methods" (1953) and "Bibliography Revisited" (1969) in his *Essays in Bibliography*, pp. 131–34, 151–95. See also G. Thomas Tanselle's "Tolerances in Bibliographical Description," *Library*, 5th ser., 23 (1968), 1–12.

²¹ "The Concept of Ideal Copy," *SB*, 33 (1980), 46 (we have reversed Tanselle's italics). Ideal copy is also discussed in Bowers, *Principles of Bibliographical Description* (1949; rpt. New York: Russell, 1962), pp. 113–23, 404–06.

²² Cited in note 17.